THE STORY AND LANGUAGE OF
HERALDRY

THE STORY AND LANGUAGE OF
HERALDRY

The development of coats of arms and
heraldic symbols, with 575 illustrations

STEPHEN SLATER

southwater

For Ma, the dogs, and the Gang of Four

This edition is published by Southwater, an imprint of Anness Publishing Ltd,
Blaby Road, Wigston, Leicestershire LE18 4SE; info@anness.com

www.southwaterbooks.com; www.annesspublishing.com

Anness Publishing has a picture agency outlet for images for publishing, promotions or advertising.
Please visit our website www.practicalpictures.com for more information.

Publisher: Joanna Lorenz
Managing Editor: Helen Sudell
Senior Editor: Joanne Rippin
Picture Research: Steve Slater and Veneta Bullen
Designer: Nigel Partridge
Cover Design: sugarfreedesign, London
Illustrations: Antony Duke, Marco Foppoli, Roland Symons and Alfred Znamierowski

© Anness Publishing Ltd 2012

A CIP catalogue record for this book is available from the British Library.

PUBLISHER'S NOTE
Although the advice and information in this book are believed to be accurate and true at the time of going
to press, neither the authors nor the publisher can accept any legal responsibility or liability for any errors
or omissions that may have been made.

Contents

ORIGINS AND DEVELOPMENT

Many theories have been put forward to account for the evolution and perfection of heraldry. Its birth coincided with changes in the nature of European society itself, which was becoming more sophisticated, with more and more estates passing from one generation to the next.

Throughout Europe, the general trend to migration that had characterized the Dark Ages had come to a halt. Family roots were now firmly bedded in, with the village settlement in place and, at its centre, the first two "estates": the priest, who prayed for all, and the knight or lord, who fought for all. By the 13th century, the notion of gentility was firmly established among the lordly classes, who sought connections with similarly genteel families through marriage. The idea of a stable, ancient and exclusive bloodline was accentuated, and the development of the shield of arms created an ideal symbol to confirm the hereditary nature of that descent.

◄ *A medieval stained glass window showing the king of France bearing a shield of arms.*

THE BIRTH OF HERALDRY

The Bayeux Tapestry, created to record the victory of William I, Duke of Normandy, at the Battle of Hastings in 1066, provides a vivid and detailed picture of 11th-century warfare. Scenes of the battle show that emblems were displayed on the shields of the Norman knights, but they are not considered to be heraldic devices, as the same knights bear different symbols in other episodes of the work.

Conventional heraldic thought puts the beginnings of heraldry a full century later, though it has been suggested that heraldic devices were actually in use on the battlefield of Hastings – not on the Norman shields, but on the standards and pennons borne by senior commanders of the Flemish contingent in Duke William's army – and even that heraldry originated among the heirs of the Emperor Charlemagne, who died in 814, two and a half centuries before the Battle of Hastings. Thirty years after Duke William's victory at Hastings,

▼ *The fanciful creatures on the shields of the knights on the Bayeux Tapestry perhaps presage the birth of heraldry.*

the Byzantine Princess Anna Comnena (1083–c1148) was casting her curious and careful eye over the shields of the Frankish knights who were passing through Byzantium on their way to join in the First Crusade. In the *Alexiad*, her journal of those far-off times, the princess mentions with much admiration that the shields of the Frankish knights were "extremely smooth and gleaming with a brilliant boss of molten brass", yet the account is most interesting for what it makes no mention of – any suggestion of personal devices or patterns such as those we describe by the term "heraldry".

EARLY HERALDIC CHARGES

In England the birth of heraldry is closely associated with the long but troubled reign of Henry I (1068–1135), known for the feuding within the royal family as its members struggled for power. An illustration in a late 12th-century manuscript of John of Worcester's Chronicle illustrates the nature of the age. As Henry lies in troubled sleep, in his nightmare he is surrounded by jostling knights, intent, it would seem, on

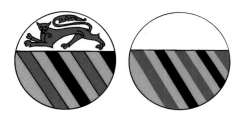

▲ *These Arabic roundels, from the time of the crusades, show a marked similarity to the early heraldry of Christian Europe.*

▲ *Personal seals often show rider and horse bearing heraldic garments, as in this fragment of the seal of the Count of St Pol, 1162.*

doing the king mischief. As well as their upraised swords, the knights bear the kite-shaped shields of their age, charged with bends, chevrons and other geometric patterns associated with early heraldry.

By the second half of the 12th century, the male members of the nobility of Europe were starting to place upon their shields certain devices, or "charges", which had become associated with their families. Symbols such as chevrons and lions appeared on their seals and military accoutrements. Some surviving seals from this period bear pictures of mounted knights carrying shields of arms, while on others the shield itself is the principal device. At the same time, the marrying of shield and symbol was starting to become hereditary. It is this splendid coupling that we recognize as heraldry.

▲ *Henry I of England having a nightmare involving knights whose shields suggest patterns soon to be adopted on heraldic shields.*

WILLIAM LONGESPÉE'S SHIELD

In 1127–8, Henry I knighted his son-in-law, Geoffrey Plantagenet, Count of Anjou, and (according to John of Marmoutier, who also wrote a chronicle of the king's reign in about 1170) on that occasion the king invested Count Geoffrey with a blue shield decorated with fanciful golden lions. Certainly such a shield is shown on Geoffrey's splendid enamel tomb-plate – taken from his burial place in Le Mans and now in the Musée de Tessé, Le Mans – but the plate and the account both date from up to 30 years after the investiture.

▼ *The effigy of William Longespée. The design of his shield of arms is almost certainly identical to that of his grandfather.*

It is certain, however, that Geoffrey's illegitimate grandson, William Longespée ("Longsword"), Earl of Salisbury and half-brother to Kings Richard I ("Coeur de Lion") and John, is depicted on his tomb in Salisbury Cathedral bearing a shield that is similar, if not identical, to that of his grandfather. Geoffrey, Count of Anjou died in 1151; William Longespée in 1226: the two depictions of their shields are usually cited as the first real evidence in colour of one shield of arms descending to another person in a hereditary manner.

ROLLS OF ARMS

Whatever the reasons for heraldry's origins – the ancient symbols borne on seals and flags, the feudal system of 12th-century Europe, the tournament, advances in armour – by the beginning of the 13th century this use of symbols had been transformed into a science of heredity, and

▲ *The tomb-plate of Geoffrey of Anjou, bearing a shield similar to the one later used by his grandson, William Longespée.*

the heralds, who were to give that science its name, had started to keep records of the shields of all that enjoyed its use. These were the splendid documents known as "rolls of arms", which were often illuminated, and which carefully recorded the retinue of some great lord, identifying the arms of all his vassals.

Many medieval rolls of arms, whether illustrated or not, list the shields of arms of men taking part in a particular event, such as a battle or tournament. Others link together groupings of knights in particular areas. Such documents provide the historian with information about the make-up of society at a period when much of Europe was forming itself into a network of nation states. One splendid surviving example is the armorial of about 1370 compiled by Claes Heinen who, as Gelre Herald, was an officer-of-arms to the Duke of Gelderland (which is now part of the Netherlands). In it, the large arms of feudal overlords are shown with the smaller arms of their vassals grouped around them. The information seems surprisingly accurate for its time, and was perhaps obtained from contacts with fellow heralds of different nations.

HERALDRY IN MEDIEVAL SOCIETY

The rise of the tournament and the refinement of the armourer's craft, which allowed the well-dressed fighting man to have his face protected behind a great iron helmet, are the two main reasons given for the explosion of armorial devices between 1150 and 1250; these twin developments also gave medieval knights ideal outlets for their peacock-like pride and natural pomposity.

The evolution of the tournament as the principal showcase for knightly prowess – apart, that is, from periods of actual warfare – assisted, even if it did not directly influence, the nature of heraldic display. This close relationship can be seen in the fact that the crest worn on top of the helmet, the second most important accoutrement in the heraldic "achievement" (the complete display of armorial bearings), was in certain countries afforded only to those of tournament rank – that is, the richest and most influential of the knightly class.

▼ *The confusion of a medieval melée is depicted in this scene from* The Book of Tourneys *by René of Anjou (1409–80).*

THE FEUDAL SYSTEM

Feudalism, from the medieval Latin word *feodum* (meaning knight's fee), as it developed in early medieval France, was not new but had evolved to cope with the troubles of the age. Since the 9th century, western Europe had been increasingly threatened by the Vikings from the north and the Muslims, Slavs and Magyars from the east. The skilled horseman, or knight, became the essential element of the western European defensive – and offensive – structure, and kings were more or less dependent on knights to provide the armoured formation needed for battle.

In return for their service to the king, the greater lords received grants of land. The lords would, in turn, parcel up their estates into smaller areas of land, each considered enough to support a knight. In his turn, the knight pledged loyalty to his lord and swore to fight for him, and consequently the monarch, whenever required. Each lord held his lands in "fief" from his overlord, and each vassal made an act of homage to his overlord, and took an oath to the effect that his possession of his estate was conditional on the service he rendered.

▲ *A stained-glass window in Chartres Cathedral, France, shows the king with his shield of arms setting out to war.*

MEDIEVAL WARFARE

When an army took to the field, the chances of any actual fighting were quite small. Towns might be besieged and villages pillaged, but for much of the time the rival forces saw little of each other. Manpower was essential to the smooth

▲ *An illustration from* The Genealogical History from Bruce to Edward I. *The shield in the centre shows an escarbuncle, a design that probably began as a shield boss.*

◄ *Duke William (middle) lifts his helmet at the Battle of Hastings to show his face.*

running of the nation and if a treaty could be brought to fruition so much the better. Great battles such as Crécy (1346), Agincourt (1415) and Towton (1461) were the exception rather than the rule. Towton, where as many as 30,000 died, took place during the Wars of the Roses, but the actual campaigning that took place during the entire period of conflict, from the first battle of St Albans in 1461 to the death of Richard III at Bosworth in 1485, amounted to only a few weeks.

When it did happen, medieval fighting was a gruesome and bloody affair, with weapons designed for hand-to-hand combat. The longsword could sever entire limbs, and the warhammer could inflict crushing and fatal blows to the head. These were the weapons of the knight and would have been too expensive for the ordinary foot soldier, who relied on weapons made by the local blacksmith, such as poleaxes, and billhooks. But these could pull a fully armed knight off his horse, or disembowel the horse to bring the knight down.

While armour gave the knight some protection, it had its disadvantages. An hour's fast fighting would be taxing for any man, but for a heavily armoured knight it could be lethal in itself. It should also be remembered that often more men died of disease while on the march between engagements than were killed in battle.

IDENTIFICATION IN BATTLE

With knights encased in armour, it is clear that armorial devices would have been exceptionally useful, both to their allies and their enemies. A scene in the Bayeux Tapestry records a moment when Duke William was forced to throw back his helmet, exposing his face for instant recognition, even though in 1066 the helmet worn by the European knight still allowed much of the wearer's face to be seen. In the mid-12th century the Anglo-Norman poet Robert Wace wrote that at Hastings the Normans "had made cognizances so that one Norman would recognize another", and the Norman French terms *connoissances* and *recognitiones*, both of which were used in the 12th century to describe armorial devices, testify to their roles as emblems of recognition. Yet there is an important fact to be remembered when reading Wace's comment – by his day, a century after Hastings, the well-dressed warrior had started to wear the great helm, which covered all of the face except for the eyes, making identification even more difficult than it would have been at the time of the Norman conquest of England.

The Genealogical History from Bruce to Edward I is a surviving manuscript from c1264-1300. It depicts medieval battle between knights who bear shields that are adorned with simple geometric patterns. One particular illustration (seen here) shows both riders and horses wearing "a coat of arms" as well as a knight banneret (top right), an oblong banner that ensured that even though a knight might not be seen, his presence on the field was evident.

▼ *Louis XII leaves for battle in 1502 dressed in full war gear, as is his horse.*

CHIVALRY AND HERALDRY

to Christianity, through prayer, preaching and writing books, one of the most influential being his *Libre del Ordre de Cavayleria (Book of the Order of Chivalry)*, written in 1275. For centuries this was considered the standard textbook on the subject and was widely translated.

Christine de Pisan (*c*1364–*c*1430), a disciple of Honoré Bonet (*fl. c*1380), provided a fascinating insight into the workings of the medieval mind in her book of 1408–9, *Le Livre des Faits d'Armes et de Chevalerie (The Book of Feats of Arms and Chivalry)*, which deals with such varied themes as banning the use of poisoned arrows by Christians, and saving the souls of warriors. She was clearly acquainted with the latest trends in military thinking in the early 15th century, and tackled questions, such as "Should the Emperor make war on the Pope?" and "Can a madman be justly held prisoner?" Her answer – "No" – to the second question displays a level of humanity uncommon in her age.

Heraldry is so closely associated with that extraordinary medieval phenomenon, chivalry, that it is instructive to explore the interplay between the two, one being very much the plaything of the other. Literally, chivalry meant the lore of the horse soldier, or rather the man who could afford the horse, its trappings and the weapons of the mounted warrior, notably the lance: in other words, the knight. At its birth, heraldry was the province of the knights; it was through the loyalty of such men that wars could be fought and won.

▲ *Medieval illustrations such as this used heraldry to depict the brotherhood of mounted knights in battle.*

Lull (*c*1232–*c*1315), an Aragonian of noble blood, was well versed in knightly deeds and wrote of love and the pursuit of it in the style of the troubadours of southern France. Amorous by nature, he often cheated on his wife, until he had a vision of Christ on the cross, which he interpreted to mean he was to change his life. His work thereafter was to convert the heathen

▼ *Christine de Pisan presenting* The Book of Feats of Arms and Chivalry *to Queen Isabeau of France.*

THE CHIVALRIC CODE
The armoured knight and his force formed the backbone of the medieval European army. If disciplined, they could turn the tide of battle, but battles were sometimes won without the combat even starting: the sight of the armoured cavalry could be enough to cause their enemies to flee.

Without battles to keep them occupied, men in fighting mood could get bored and become a liability to the ruler, his people and the Church. Something was needed to curb the semi-legalized vandalism of marauding knights and it evolved in the form of the nebulous set of ethics now called the "code of chivalry", which gradually refined into a loose set of rules aimed at civilizing the high-born. It was a theme picked up by writers of the time, including Raymond Lull, Honoré Bonet and Christine de Pisan.

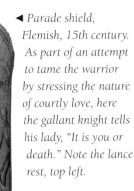

◀ *Parade shield, Flemish, 15th century. As part of an attempt to tame the warrior by stressing the nature of courtly love, here the gallant knight tells his lady, "It is you or death." Note the lance rest, top left.*

Drawing on such diverse sources as Roman military strategy and the love songs and martial epics of the German *Minnesinger* and French troubadours, Lull, de Pisan and others attracted the attention of the rulers of Europe, most of whom sought to make their courts centres of learning and chivalric enterprise. They also hoped that through such pursuits as courtly love, tournaments and orders of chivalry, they would pacify their unruly courtiers and weld them into a coherent force that saw loyalty to the overlord as a benefit rather than a hindrance.

In its simplest form the code required that its followers should honour their lord, defend the Church – including, when possible, taking up arms against the infidel – and protect the weak, the poor and all women. In reality, true followers of such noble aims were rare, and even those warriors who were held up by medieval writers and the Church as paragons of chivalry would today be looked upon in a very different light.

It says much of those times that one of the men who most epitomized the code of chivalry was not a Christian knight at all, but the infidel ruler Saladin (1137–93), Sultan of Egypt and Syria, who led the Muslim army against the Crusaders in Palestine. As for that most Christian monarch, Richard Coeur de Lion, his observation of the code was less punctilious: in 1191, over 2,500 prisoners in the captured garrison of Acre were put to the sword, for little reason other than Saladin had not observed the treaty between himself and Richard "to the word".

LOVE AND HERALDRY

Heraldry had a great part to play in chivalric ideals. The winning of a good lady through love and brave quests was a popular theme, and books were liberally scattered with allegorical arms. Often medieval chroniclers used the castle as a symbol of a lady's virtue that was to be stormed and captured by the knight's love and passion.

The most delightful depictions of shields of arms appear in a unique survival from about 1300, the Manesse Codex, now in the University of Heidelberg. This collection of songs is illustrated with no less than 140 miniatures showing knightly troubadours – each identified by his shield – preparing for a tournament, sighing for love or wooing a mistress.

▲ *A scene from the Manesse Codex in which the victor receives his prize (a jewelled chaplet) from the Queen of the Tournament.*

▲ *A depiction in ivory of knights assaulting the castle of love.*

MEDIEVAL MILITARY DRESS

Heraldry grew up during a period of radical changes in the dress of the military man and, as those changes took place, so did the nature of heraldry, or rather its application. In time, heraldry even came to be thought of as another weapon in the warrior's armoury – it could, and did, win or lose battles. So important to each other were the twin subjects of heraldry and armour, that not only did the terms "armory" and "armour" combine, but actual pieces of armour were often represented on shields, in crests and as heraldic badges.

CHAIN MAIL

In the late 12th century, when heraldry started to appear on the battlefield, the high-ranking military man was largely

◄ An illustration of the tomb effigy of William Longespée, showing the knightly gear that would render him anonymous but for his shield and tunic.

encased in chain mail. Mail had been used by the Romans, who called it *macula*, meaning a net or mesh. Each link in medieval chain mail was forged of iron wire, the ends of which were hammered flat and riveted after the ring had been linked through four others. A chain mail shirt that has survived from the 15th century weighs around 9kg (20lb).

The later application of iron and steel plate tended to give better protection against the bruising blows of war hammer and sword, but chain mail was surprisingly good at keeping out ordinary arrows, and at the Battle of Arsouf in 1191, during the Third Crusade, Richard Coeur de Lion's men were said to have survived in spite of arrows sticking out of their mail like so many bird's feathers.

Long after mail had ceased to be the main form of body armour, it was still being used as flexible "in-filling" at points of the body where mobility was needed, such as behind the knees or under the arms, and plate armour could not be worn. Underneath the mail, a quilted undergarment called a "gambeson" was worn, which was padded with wadding: old rags, horsehair or bunches of dried grass – anything that would keep the wearer insulated, both from any extreme weather and the blows of an enemy.

▲ The typical military dress of a medieval crusader c1250. The loose-fitting tunic was an ideal surface for the display of heraldry.

► A 15th-century chain mail shirt, a highly effective piece of protection.

PLATE ARMOUR

Gradually the knight laid off his chain mail in favour of iron or steel plate and, as the armourer found ways to provide more complex and composite armour, each piece acquired its own name. The chest and back were protected by the "cuirass". Legs were enclosed in "cuisses", elbows were protected by "couters" or "gard-de-bras" (the badge of Lord Fitzwalter), hands were enclosed in gauntlets or "mains-de-fer", the neck was guarded by an "aventail" (the badge of Lord Montague), and the shoulders sported plates known as "ailettes", bearing the arms of the wearer.

BADGES FROM ARMOUR

These are some of the pieces of armour that were taken up as badges by medieval knights.

▲ A gard-de-bras, worn on the elbow. *▲ A chamfron, worn by a knight's horse.*

▲ An aventail, worn at the neck.

▲ The closed helmet. *▲ A crampet, for the end of a scabbard.*

Iron and steel were not the only materials used for armour. "Plastics" (a general term for materials that could be moulded into shape) included "cuir-bouilli" (leather boiled in oil), bone and even cow-horn. The last, when heated, could be unravelled into translucent sheets and was sometimes also used as a cheap alternative to window glass, showing the ingenuity of the late medieval artisan. Leg guards, which were known as "greaves", shoulder-guards and even arm-guards could all be made of such materials. By the middle of the 14th century the linen surcoat had been largely superseded by the "jupon", a close-fitting quilted coat, usually decorated with the bearer's arms.

The great armour manufacturing areas of the 15th and 16th centuries were northern Italy – notably Milan – Nuremberg and the Low Countries. Military men living outside these areas who wanted the best had several options open to them. If they were very rich they might employ their own armourer. Failing this, they could purchase armour from travelling salesmen who visited the leading trading centres. The third option was to have a model made of their torso and limbs, in wax or wood, which could be sent to an armourer for measuring and fitting, and records in royal and noble archives bear testimony to this practice. A letter of 16 March 1520,

▼ *A tabarded knight at prayer depicted in glass, England, 1403.*

▲ *By the end of the 15th century, knights were discarding the heraldic surcoat in order to display their armour.*

◄ *The arms of Nuremberg, used here as an armourer's mark in the 15th century.*

from François I of France, asks that an "arming doublet" (an undergarment) belonging to Henry VIII of England be sent as a size guide for a new cuirass, which François wished to present to the English king.

By the end of the 15th century the well-dressed knight was encased almost entirely in steel plating, the brightness of which gave it the name of "alwyte" (all white). From the details of its lines and flutings, curves and edgings – just as today with the cut of a good suit – those in the know were able to tell where and even by whom the armour had been made. In addition, the manufacturer would have signed the plate with his punched maker's mark, which was sometimes heraldic. By the end of the 15th century the surcoat, tabard and jupon had all become things of the past, for the armour itself was what was being shown off.

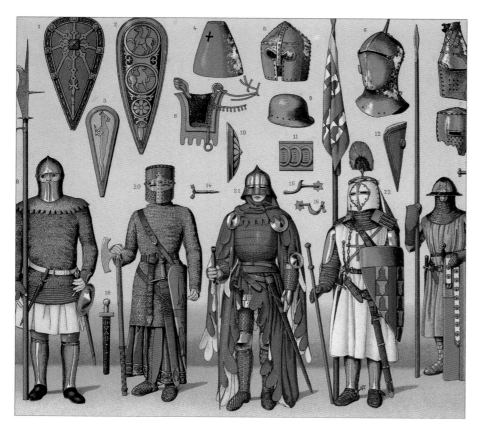

▲ *A depiction of changes and adaptations in styles of armour and accoutrements from the 12th century to the 15th century.*

FIGHTING IN ARMOUR

Needless to say, armour, whether chain mail or steel plate, was not the most comfortable of coverings. In hot weather the knight could literally cook, while in winter he might freeze. Commanders often had to berate their men during battle for taking off vital pieces of armour, in an attempt to keep cool. Many a medieval treatise on warfare pleaded for caution among the knightly classes. It might be freezing cold, it might be unbearably hot (especially in Palestine), but on no account should you discard your armour: discomfort was far preferable to death.

Some measure of comfort would have been gained by the wearing of a doublet (a long-sleeved tunic reaching to the hips) and long hose, like tights. At points that needed to be flexible but also required protection, mail was attached to the material. The underside of the armour was lined with fine materials. As for the weight of armour, it is a fact that a full harness of plate armour of about 1470 was no heavier – in fact it was sometimes lighter – than the full marching kit of a British infantryman of World War I. Furthermore, a fully armoured knight could mount his steed easily and without the aid of the crane seen in old films.

▶ *A tilt helmet, from the 15th–16th centuries, also known as the "frog face".*

FASHIONS IN HELMETS

The head, being the most vulnerable part of the body to attack, had long been protected in war by some form of metal headgear. By the time the heraldic story started, the most popular form of helmet for the warrior in Britain and other European countries was a pointed conical iron helmet with a nose-guard, similar in form to those shown in the Bayeux Tapestry. This design allowed much of the bearer's face to be seen. Gradually the helmet lost its conical point and a flat plate of iron was riveted across the top of the head. More and more of the face became protected behind iron plating, and this style is known as the "pot helmet".

At this period, around 1200, most of the body was protected by chain mail, which would also have extended over the wearer's neck, hair and the sides of the face. It was made bearable by a cloth lining, which was probably padded. Over the mail head-covering a cloth cap would have been worn, also reinforced by padding. The helmet would have sat upon this "arming cap", which gave some degree of comfort to the wearer as well as acting as a shock absorber for any blows on the helmet. Further comfort was given by air holes cut in the side of the helmet.

Although some armorial devices made an appearance on the helmet as early as 1250, it was almost another century before the

▲ *An English great helm, c1370.*

▲ *A barred tourney helm, 16th century.*

▲ Walter von Hohenklingen's tomb effigy. In death he chose to be depicted with all the accoutrements of his knightly rank, including tourney helm and shield of arms.

heraldic crest became popular. The pot helmet gradually evolved into the "great helm", made with a series of hammered plates usually rising to a gradual point.

A second, close-fitting helmet was made to fit under the great helm so that the knight now wore two layers of iron, and this in turn evolved separately, with or without a visor. This streamlined helmet, known as the "bascinet", was so popular with medieval knights that it was worn in various forms from around 1330 to 1550. It covered only the top of the head and the sides of the face, and chain mail was attached to its lower edges by cords. When the great helm, which tended to be relegated to the tournament, was worn over the bascinet each was cushioned from the other by a padded lining.

It was the great helm that became the main platform for the heraldic crest, which was usually made of lightweight materials such as hollow wood, paste board, stiffened cloth or leather stretched over a wooden or wire frame and filled with a combination of materials including tow, sawdust or even sponge. Both the bascinet and the great helm can be seen on the grave slab of Walter von Hohenklingen, in the Swiss National Museum, Zurich.

HORSE ARMOUR AND TRAPPINGS

The knight was a mounted warrior, and his horse was a valuable commodity that also needed its own protection. This led to the steed having its own "chamfron" or head-guard (the badge of the Earl of Shrewsbury) and "peytrel" or chest-plate. The horse could be dressed overall in the fashion of the day with a splendid "trapper" bearing the owner's arms. This was an embroidered cloth that reached down to the fetlocks, leaving only the horse's eyes, ears and nose uncovered. Its cost could be the equivalent of £20,000 ($30,000) today.

By the mid-14th century the combination of the skilled arts of the armourer and the embroiderer meant that Sir Geoffrey Luttrell could enter the lists dressed in a display of heraldic grandeur in which his personal arms appeared on no less than 17 separate displays.

HERALDRY BITES THE BULLET

Many surviving pieces of late harness show a proof mark: a bullet "bruise" in some inconspicuous place, by which the armourer had proved that the plate could withstand the shot of handguns. Firearms, increasingly used towards the end of the 15th century, are not respecters of rank or person, and were fired at a distance, which rendered heraldic identification superfluous. By 1500 the great age of heraldry on the battlefield was over. From then on it was used as an indicator of blood lines, marriage connections and degree (status).

▼ Sir Geoffrey Luttrell, preparing for tourney, from the Luttrell Psalter, 14th century. Sir Geoffrey's arms appear 17 times.

THE TOURNAMENT

running battles. The knights and their entourages fought violently with each other through town and village street at great risk of serious injury, not only to themselves but also to innocent locals, who were considered totally expendable.

Tournaments, "those games overseen by the devil", were railed against by religious men from the earliest days. As early as the 9th century, Pope Eugenius anathematized them, and a succession of popes attempted to ban tournaments, even going so far as excommunicating the participants. Their preachings usually had little or no effect. It is easy to see why the popes saw tournaments as the work of Satan, as some of Christendom's finest military leaders fell on the tourney field: men who, if they did have to fight their fellows to the death, the

War, which was never far from men's minds in the heyday of heraldry, needed training for. Archers had their practices at the butts, but military commanders pitted their skills against each other on the tourney field. Martial sports of some kind have surely existed from the earliest days of organized fighting. The Greeks and Romans made full use of military sparring matches and contests of strength and courage and so it was in the medieval period. This rough type of military "play" often so closely resembled real battle conditions that it often resulted in casualties – even deaths. If there was any difference between the tournament melée and the medieval battle, it was the involvement of judges, who attempted to bring some semblance of order to the motley business. Another difference was the weapons, which tended to be slightly less lethal than those used in warfare.

ORGANIZED MAYHEM

It is easy to imagine the medieval tournament as having all the atmosphere of a modern fair and sporting event combined. This may have been true when tournaments became formalized, but in the early days such events were more akin to

▲ *Tournament participants and audience at the lists, from a late 15th-century illustration of Froissart's* Chronicles.

▼ *A 16th-century tournament with broken lances littering the field. By this time the tournaments were more closely regulated.*

clerics felt should have aimed their aggression at the infidels in the Holy Land. Florent, Count of Hainault, and Philip, Count of Boulogne, were both killed on the tourney field in 1223, and as late as 1559 Henri II of France was mortally wounded during a joust, when his visor was pierced by the lance of Gabriele de Montmorency. Henri died in an age when the tournament was supposedly a formal and disciplined affair; certainly by the 16th century it had become somewhat more refined than the tournament that was held in 1240 at Nuys, near Cologne, when it is recorded that 60 knights and squires perished, trampled under horses' hooves, choked by dust in their armour, or simply succumbing to exhaustion.

TOURNAMENT EVENTS

The tournament was a series of contests reflecting the types of warfare enacted by the higher military ranks. The "melée" was the event that most closely aped the style of fighting that the combatants would probably encounter on a real battlefield. It more nearly resembled a mounted rugby scrum than any genteel sparring match. In the battle engagement, any number of mounted men slugged it out with swords, maces and other hand-held weapons.

Jousting was counted the most noble and prestigious sport to be enjoyed on the tourney field. In this, two mounted knights

▲ *A painting of a tournament in Siena in honour of Ferdinand I de' Medici, with the arms of participants and nobility displayed.*

▼ *The perils of jousting are shown clearly in this depiction of the death of King Henri II of France in 1559 at a tournament in honour of Philip II of Spain.*

bearing lances would run against each other in the "lists", an area enclosed by fences. In the early 15th century, to offset the increased danger of longer, heavier lances, a wooden barrier (the "tilt") was introduced to divide the course, with one man on either side of it.

Along the edge of the jousting field lay the spectators' enclosures and the tented encampments of the participants, all ablaze with heraldry. All the participants vied with each other in putting on the greatest display of splendour. They would be announced to the crowds by their heralds shouting out their names and titles, and often their arms would be shown to the crowds by men or boys dressed up as monsters, angels, ancient heroes or giants – surely a possible origin of the heraldic supporters of later days. With a blast of trumpets, the two knights would course towards each other, urging their horses to

▲ *The breaking of lances during the clash of contestants. Note the lance tips or coronels that were used for jousts* à la plaisance.

▼ *This event held in Rome for the Vatican Court in 1565 shows the extravagant splendour of the 16th-century tournament.*

build up the maximum speed possible in the area of the lists, which might be 200m (220 yards) or more. The clash of men and weapons, when it came, could be dramatic and, despite being mounted in a high-backed saddle, a knight could often be catapulted into the air by the force of his opponent's lance.

A joust would usually be *à la plaisance* ("of peace"), using lances with special blunted tips, called coronels. The lances were often made of hollow wood, so that they would shatter on impact. If, however, a grudge match, or joust *à outrance* ("to the end"), had been commanded, all was for real, with sharpened weapons. The competition carried on to the point where one man was either injured or killed.

The matches were closely monitored by the judge, who notched up tallies of broken lances, and at the end of the competition the winner might be awarded a prize. This could be anything from a ring, a gold chain, or a jewel, to a kiss from the "Queen of the Tournament", one of the ladies present who was chosen to reign over the proceedings. The ceremony of prize-giving could be both formal and glorious, with the prize handed over to the Queen of the day by a herald. The winner was ceremoniously brought forward and the prize presented by the Queen, with suitably gracious words of esteem.

▼ *The gorgeous apparel of a tourney knight and his horse was hugely expensive.*

THE COST OF TOURNEYING

The tournaments could make or break competitors. One of the complaints of the popes and other senior prelates against these events – beside the fact that they led to the maiming and death of many fine men – was that the heavy expense of participation led to the ruin of large numbers of poorer knights, who often pawned all their belongings, and even their estates, to finance their entry into the lists. But if a knight was prepared to take the risk, the rewards could set him on the road to greater things. And there was certainly money to be made at the tournament.

One such professional knight was William Marshal (1146–1219), who eventually served as adviser to no less than four English kings and was created Earl of

▲ *The effigy of William Marshal, of whom it was written, "Behold all that remains of the best knight that ever lived."*

Pembroke. William was born into a good family, but the Marshal estates were devolved upon his older brothers. He was therefore expected to find his own way in the world, and did so in successful and dramatic fashion.

Apprenticed to William de Tancarville's household in Normandy, William Marshal was a quick learner in the ways of the medieval martial man. When, in a melée at a tournament in Maine, the young William gained the capture of three knights through his own prowess, he saw the way his life was to run. As in a real battle, it was ransom that could make or break a man's

▲ *Unsuitable for battle, the full regalia a knight wore for tournaments was for identification and to show his wealth and position.*

fortune. With the money and horses William won that day he was able to join the ever-growing number of knights who wandered round Europe from tourney to tourney, making good use of their fighting skills to amass wealth and increase their own prestige. These roving warriors attracted other such men to their side, and grew into a force of professional military men who came to form the backbone of many of medieval Europe's armies.

In 1167 he teamed up with a Flemish knight, Roger de Gaugi, agreeing to take part in as many tournaments as they could and divide the ransom spoils between them. William continued to take part in tournaments until 1183, and remained undefeated throughout 16 years of competition. Later, on his death bed, he recalled that he had taken over 500 knights prisoner during those years. Such was the life of the tournament roundsman.

THE FIELD OF CLOTH OF GOLD

Tournaments provided the major aristocracy and royalty of Europe with an arena in which they could show off their wealth and largesse. By the 15th century kings were keen to be the patrons of these gaudy and glorious shows. Marriages, coming of age, truces, treaties and alliances: all were seen as possible excuses for a tournament, the medieval equivalent of the ultimate party. The most incredible spectacle of this kind took place in 1520 and came to be known as the Field of Cloth of Gold.

It was a meeting at Guines in June 1520, between François I of France and Henry VIII of England, arranged to celebrate a peace between the two nations. For once, instead of fighting each other, each monarch attempted to outdo the other with a show of magnificence. Although other events were organized, the tournaments were the main excitements of the week. The participants were housed in two encampments, each with over 1,000 lavishly decorated tents. Between the two camps stood the Tree of Chivalry. This extraordinary structure bore the shields of the two monarchs, bound together by garlands of green silk. The tree's trunk was covered in cloth of gold and at its foot, in complete harmony, stood the heralds of both kingdoms.

▼ *A painting showing the famous tournament, the Field of Cloth of Gold, at the moment of the extravagant entry of Henry VIII of England, on 7 June 1520.*

THE ROMANTIC REVIVAL

Tournaments became few and far between in the first half of the 17th century, and seem to have died a natural death by the 1650s. There was a brief renaissance in the first half of the 19th century, when members of the European aristocracy, bowled over by the Romantic revival of medievalism, which included the historical romances of Sir Walter Scott, saw themselves as the proud and natural successors to Parsifal, the Swan Knight, and to Arthur and the Knights of the Round Table.

It was in Scott's own Scotland that the last great attempt at re-creating the medieval chivalric ideal was staged, to celebrate the coronation of the young Queen Victoria in 1837. The coronation was a toned-down affair, shorn of many of its more splendid trappings by a thrifty Whig government. This caused particular resent-ment in one young Scottish aristocrat, Archibald Montgomerie, 13th Earl of Eglinton. His stepfather had been one of those Tory gentlemen who considered themselves deprived of their rightful, if small, parts in the coronation ritual by Whig penny-pinching. As a lover of chivalry, Lord Eglinton decided to right the wrong done to him and his family. He could and would provide the chivalric splendour worthy of his race – he would revive the tournament.

The grand event was held at the Earl's estate at Eglinton, south of Glasgow. Lord Eglinton's enthusiasm fired many other noble souls into wanting to revive their family's fame – that is, until they realized the actual expense involved and the training and degree of expertise required for the event. So out of the original 150 entrants expected, only 13 knights actually turned

▲ *One of the contemporary illustrations of the Eglinton Tournament shows the procession of Lord Eglinton and other participants.*

out for the tournament. However, this in no way deterred the crowds that came to witness the fun. An estimated 100,000 people turned up but, as is so often the case, the British weather decided to stop play. The rain came down in buckets, turning the lists into a quagmire.

Although ridiculed by many at the time for its fanciful attempts at re-creating a golden age, which in reality never existed, what was truly amazing was that Lord Eglinton's attempts were probably as true to the 15th-century tourney scene as anything attempted since that period itself.

▼ *The breaking of lances during the jousting at the Eglinton Tournament.*

BADGES AND LIVERIES

In medieval Britain, most of the populace would not have known the arms of even the greatest magnate, but they would quite probably have recognized the badge (also known as a cognizance) – the distinguishing emblem of the major nobility – as well as the liveries, or clothing, that were worn by their servants.

BADGES

The badge is a particularly British heraldic tradition but is also known in Italy, where nobility were represented by devices, known as *imprese* or "impresses". The badge became fashionable in England in the late 14th century. The emblem used could be a single charge taken from the arms of the owner or, as was often the case, it might be an entirely different object chosen at the will of the bearer. As such it was very personal, and in certain great families various members would possess their own badge, quite distinct from those of their relations. Some families made use of many different devices: Richard II of England's favourites were the white hart and the "broom cod", as it was called – the seed pod of the broom plant. It is thought that a sprig of broom (in Latin *planta genista*) had given the name Plantagenet to his line.

Badges were particularly associated with the struggles for power between two royal houses, which later came to be known as the Wars of the Roses (1455–85). This

◄ *A rare surviving pewter badge, from the late 14th to early 15th century, of the "broom cod" device of Richard II of England.*

name was coined later from the supposed badges of the rival royal houses of York (the white rose) and Lancaster (the red rose). During this period of civil disorder, the retinues of the major nobility amounted to private armies, whose members would wear their master's badge and colours or "livery" to declare their allegiance. The sight of the badge could instil either comfort or fear in the minds of the peasantry, depending on which device they saw – it might belong to the troops of their own lord, or might be that of some mighty rival. Bands of armed men roving around the country, intent on mischief, were a phenomenon of the age. In this atmosphere,

◄ *The badges and personal liveries of (top to bottom) King Edward III, Richard II and Henry IV from Writhe's* Garter Book.

▼ *A carving of the salamander, the badge of François I of France (1515–47).*

▲ *A splendid and rare survival of the silver crescent, badge of the Percy family, Earls of Northumberland. This example dates from the early 15th century.*

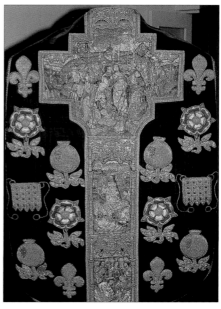

▲ *Worked into this chasuble are the combined badges of Henry VIII (the Tudor rose and portcullis) and Catherine of Aragon (the pomegranate), celebrating their marriage.*

wearing the badge of a particular lord gave some degree of immunity from prosecution in the local court, since the chances were that the magistrate was also in the pay of the same magnate.

THE BATTLE OF BARNET

The white mullet, or star, of the de Veres was partially responsible for one famous defeat during the Wars of the Roses. In 1471, Richard Neville, Earl of Warwick, the former friend and supporter of the Yorkist king Edward IV, was fighting against him, having now sided with his Lancastrian rival, Henry VI. The two armies met at Barnet. The royal troops wore the rising sun of York; Warwick's forces were wearing red tunics upon which was the white ragged staff. (The bear and the ragged staff of Lancaster were, initially,

two separate badges, combined only in later centuries.)

On that day Warwick was joined by the troops of John de Vere, Earl of Oxford. At the height of the battle, which was fought in thick mist, de Vere's forces managed to drive the Yorkists backwards. After this success they attempted to rejoin the main Lancastrian force, and appeared out of the mist at some distance from their colleagues. Warwick's archers, mistaking the

star on Lord Oxford's badge for the Yorkist sunburst, believed they were being attacked by King Edward's men, and let loose a shower of arrows. Oxford's troops believed that their former comrades had turned traitor and what had lately seemed destined to be a Lancastrian victory soon turned into a shambolic defeat for them. Warwick was killed and King Edward was able to march on to Tewkesbury and complete the defeat of King Henry's cause.

▶ *The tomb effigy of Sir Richard Herbert, who wears the famous Yorkist collar of suns and roses.*

LIVERY

Personal liveries could take the form of robes in a lord's colours (these did not necessarily have to be the same colours used in his arms), the wearing of his badge, or badges, and in some cases among the greater nobility, a collar. Such livery collars tended to differ slightly in the metal they were made of, depending on the rank of the wearer. The collar of interlocking "Ss" of the House of Lancaster was used by Henry IV, who granted the right to wear it to individuals as a mark of his favour, and it is still being worn in England to this day, notably by the heralds and kings of arms.

Various monarchs attempted to curb the powers of the rival nobles by passing statutes against the wearing of liveries and the maintenance of private armies. Richard II's statute of 1390 was prompted by these practices, and was aimed at those "…Who wore the badges of lords…so swollen with pride that no fear would deter them from committing extortion in their shires."

Other complainants at the time bemoaned those "Officers of great men that weareth the liveries, the which…robbeth and despoileth the poor", and "hats and liveries…by the granting of which a lord could induce his neighbours to maintain him in all his quarrels, whether reasonable or not." Richard II responded with an ordinance that aimed at inhibiting lords from "giving livery of company to anyone unless he is a family servant living in the household." Exceptions were made for some

▲ *A depiction in stained glass of a banner-bearer for the Swiss city and canton of Berne, from the first half of the 16th century.*

▼ *Richard II portrayed in the* Wilton Diptych *of 1395, in which he wears his personal badges – a white hart and broom cods.*

▼ *The collar of an English herald – the Ss are a survival from the livery collar of the House of Lancaster.*

lords, but later monarchs continued to try to curb the power of the nobles by statutes of livery and maintenance.

As late as the reign of Henry VII, the king exercised such statutes (in 1495 and 1504) and could even apply them to his most trusted friends and admirers, as when he visited John de Vere at Castle Hedingham. Henry was led by his host to the castle through two lines of the earl's numerous servants, each wearing coats of their master's livery. The king berated his host for exceeding the limits laid down respecting the number of household retainers, saying "My lord, I have heard much of your hospitality, but I see it is greater than the speech...I may not endure to have my laws broken in my sight. My attorney must speak with you." A hefty fine was soon demanded.

▲ *The* impresa *of the Rusconi family – an ice crampon – is an apt device for a family based in the mountains of north Italy.*

▲ *One of the many badges, combining device and motto, used by the Visconti family, Dukes of Milan, in the 15th century.*

STATUTORY UNIFORMS

As well as the statutory attempts that were made to limit the wearing of liveries, laws were enacted throughout Europe to curb the populace's entitlement to wear certain furs, jewels or styles of dress. In numerous states, specific groups of people were made

▼ *An illustration from one of the books of ready-made* imprese *designs.*

to wear certain items of dress, or to have some sign to indicate their social status.

In 15th-century Germany the women in a layman's family had to wear a yellow veil. European Jews often had to wear a yellow patch – a theme taken up some five centuries later by the Nazis – and prostitutes were distinguished by a number of modes of dress, depending on their age and the country in which they lived. In the time of Charles V of France (1364–80), prostitutes had to wear on their arm a ribbon different to the colour of their dress.

IMPRESE

In northern Italy from the late 14th century onwards it was customary for the greater nobility to maintain *imprese*. These were badges that were usually accompanied by a personal motto or phrase. Families such as the Rusconis of Valtellina had just one *impresa*, an ice crampon. Ruling dynasties made use of many. The theme of the personal *impresa* on the

Italian model was later taken up by the jousting fraternities of France and England, who consulted poets and allegorical story-writers to achieve a suitable combination of badge and motto. Often, such an armorial marriage would exist for just one tournament or pageant, being discarded at will by the bearer. The noble warrior clearly had to have his wits about him if he wanted to achieve on each occasion a new and effective device, but help was at hand by way of books written by designers of these curiosities of conceit. The furnishing of a new *imprese* for every occasion was an expensive business, and it gradually diminished in popularity as the tournament declined in the 17th century.

MODERN BADGES

In England, the badge has been enjoying a comeback since 1906, when heralds started granting them again, together with the standard. It has been suggested that the marrying of badge and standard for modern-day armigers is illogical, because it presumes that they have a following in the medieval manner. On this basis, the standard and its "badge" should be granted only to institutions, such as schools and colleges. Nevertheless, the granting of a badge along with a new coat of arms to an individual had become commonplace at the English College of Arms by the end of the 20th century.

HERALDIC FLAGS

There is surely no more emotive symbol of belonging than a flag or standard. Such objects of attention are as old as history itself. Heraldry has appeared upon flags almost from its very start. There is a suggestion that heraldic designs make an early appearance in the Bayeux Tapestry, on the flags, pennons or guidons of the Flemish contingent in Duke William's army. On the opposing side, the "wyvern" or two-legged dragon of Wessex is held high by King Harold's standard-bearer. The lance pennons of Normans and Flemings at Hastings were obviously made of cloth, but it would seem that the standard of Wessex was carved in wood or metal.

▶ *A Renaissance interpretation of Roman standard-bearers graphically illustrates the rousing effects of flags.*

▼ *Part of the medieval Powell Roll of Arms, c1345, showing designs for the banners of high-ranking English commanders.*

Whatever the materials, both armies made use of "flags" of some sort on that fateful day, and almost certainly they were meant as objects of veneration, both for individuals and for entire units.

KNIGHTS BANNERET

One type of flag, the banner, gave its name to a class of medieval military men, the knights banneret, or bannerets for short. These high-ranking commanders were able to bring a body of men to a battle under their own banner – a square or oblong flag bearing the knight's own arms. (In the 12th and 13th centuries the banner tended to have a width one-third of its length, whereas in later centuries it became square.) The banner was a most important indicator to the troops of their commander's presence on the field of battle. Held high above the banneret's head, the banner went wherever he did, and the two

▶ *A funeral banner* (Totenfahne) *of the Swiss Counts von Toggenburg, c1436.*

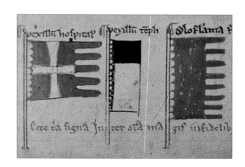

▲ *Banners of the Knights Hospitallers and Templar, and the Oriflamme of France.*

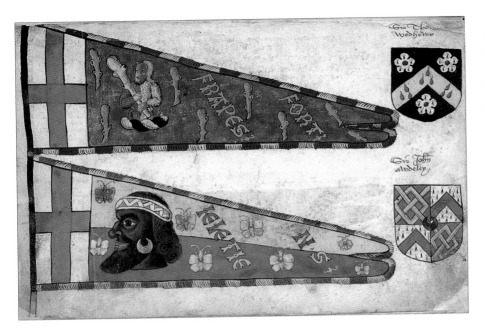

The most famous flag of this type was the Oriflamme of France, which was kept for centuries in the Abbey of Saint Denis (the burial place of the French royal family). Various suggestions have been made as to the exact appearance of the Oriflamme, but it would seem to have been made of red silk with golden trimmings, and hung from a staff of gilded wood or metal: hence its name, which means "golden flame". Some accounts say that the Oriflamme was last seen in use at Agincourt (1415), where its bearer, William Martel, Seigneur de Baqueville, lost his life defending it. Other chroniclers say it remained in the Abbey of Saint Denis until at least the 18th century, when it was described as being in a very unkempt state.

▲ *Standards of English nobility from the first half of the 16th century, each with the cross of St George in hoist.*

were seldom separated, unless through the death of the banner-bearer.

The banneret could be so created on the battlefield as a reward for his bravery. Prior to that moment, he would probably have been a bachelor or "bas chevalier", a lower knight who bore as his rank a long pennon that had a triangular tail or tails, with his arms in a panel near the pole. Whoever was in overall command that day – a king, prince or other commander – would indicate his appreciation by taking the knight's pennon and cutting away the tails, thus making it into a banner.

The banneret had some special prerogatives. In France, he could place a banner-shaped weathervane above his castle, and could also choose his own *cri-de-guerre* or war cry. In the Low Countries, he had a circlet or coronet of rank in his crest.

PENNONS AND STANDARDS
Two other types of heraldic flag were popular with the knightly class. One was the pennon, a triangular flag that could bear either arms or a badge. The other was the standard, a long tapering flag, larger than the pennon, which could have a split or rounded end. Instead of the bearer's arms, the standard tended to show the badge or

device of the bearer. This could appear singly or several times, and was often accompanied by the motto or *cri-de-guerre*. The "hoist" of the standard (the area at the top of the flag near the pole) tended to bear the national device. The main background to the standard was made up of the livery colours of the bearer. While a knight bachelor was entitled to bear a standard but not a banner, a banneret was entitled to both.

THE GONFALONE
Flags are, of course, not the exclusive preserve of the nobility. The military places great importance on regimental colours, and in the Catholic Church the position of gonfalonier, or standard-bearer, of the Church, was one of the most prestigious offices the pope could bestow.

The office of gonfalonier takes its name from another type of flag popular among city states and other nations during the medieval period, the gonfalone. Such flags were often of huge size and bore many tails. They were carried hanging down from a cross beam, rather like the sail of a ship. Before a battle the gonfalone was blessed by the clergy and it was a great disgrace to lose it, for some were considered to have miraculous powers. Because of its size, a gonfalone was often borne on a cart, driven by a member of a particular family for whom the post was hereditary.

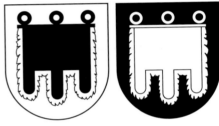

▲ *The characteristic shape of the gonfalone itself became a heraldic charge, perhaps adopted by families whose ancestors had been the hereditary bearers.*

▼ *A carroccio (flag cart) from the arms of the Grulli family, hereditary carroccio drivers to the city of Florence.*

HERALDS
AND THE LAW
OF ARMS

By the 15th century, heralds had become the acknowledged experts in everything associated with arms, and from that time the study and "noble science of arms" became known as heraldry. As with all matters of heraldry, the law of arms has varied widely depending on time and place, and medieval writers differed in their opinions concerning who should and should not bear arms. Some contested that only those of noble stock had such a right, while others suggested that anyone should be able to assume them. The matter continues to be debated among heraldists, though most governments now take little interest in it, apart from enshrining somewhere in law their people's right to adopt arms at will, and for those who have done so to protect their arms in the same manner as a surname.

◀ *A beautifully restored German Totenschild,*
or death shield, for a member of the Jörg
family of Nördlingen.

MEDIEVAL HERALDS

The term "herald" seems to have its origins in the Old German word *beer-wald*, suggesting a caller or proclaimer to the army. Certainly, early references to heralds in French medieval romances seem to suggest they shared a common ancestry with the minstrels and messengers of noble households. Other 12th- and 13th-century writers refer to freelance individuals who followed the newly fashionable sport of tourneying across Europe, employed to cry out the names of knights and recount their lineage and acts of prowess.

Heralds took an interest in matters armorial. At tournaments, and in battle, the heralds needed to recognize and memorize the arms of the participants, and for this purpose they compiled pictorial rolls of armorial bearings. (Rolls of arms were initially actual rolls of parchment or vellum, but the term also came to be used to describe armorial records in book form.) Some rolls, known as "ordinaries", were classified by all the different devices, or charges, that could be placed on a shield.

MEMBERS OF THE HOUSEHOLD

By the end of the 13th century heralds had become attached to noble households, where they were employed as messengers, proclaiming challenges for forthcoming tournaments on their lords' behalf. It would seem that a herald was still allowed

▲ *The herald of the Duke of Brittany, wearing the ermine tabard of his master, shows the Duke of Bourbon the arms of contenders in a tournament.*

▼ *A 15th-century herald with the banners of the judges overseeing a tournament.*

to journey for some length of time away from the household, amassing information on the tourney and all that was associated with chivalry; for if his lord wanted to be seen as a man of quality he was expected to be well acquainted in such matters.

Originally the freelance heralds had taken their titles at will, but as they became accredited to certain noble households they took their official names from their masters' own titles or badges, or from charges that appeared in their arms: Toison d'or ("golden fleece") was the herald of the Burgundian order of that name; Montjoie took his name from the *cri-de-guerre* of the French kings, "Mont joie de Saint Denis"; and the name Blanch Sanglier ("white boar") came from the personal badge of Richard Duke of Gloucester, later Richard III. Heralds themselves do not normally figure on family arms, but the Spanish family of de Armas, which descends from

the herald Juan Negrin, king of arms to the kings of Castile, bears on its shield an arm holding a banner charged with the arms of the kingdoms of Castile and León.

Early references to the herald were often none too complimentary: perhaps they were written by minstrels who saw themselves under threat from these men who

▼ *The arms of the de Armas family, which contain an unusual charge alluding to their ancestor's position as a king of arms.*

vied for their masters' attention. One late 13th-century poet, Henri de Laon, thought that the herald pursued an idle profession, worthy only of greedy men: "What's more, lords would give shelter to up to four of these ne'er-do-wells who tended to talk more than good folk of other callings, yet at the same time do very little."

By the late 14th century the herald had advanced to become a permanent fixture in the households of royalty and the major nobility – to help in organizing tournaments or to act as a personal emissary. While lesser nobles might have only one herald, the households of ruling dukes, princes and kings were more likely to contain a formal heraldic staff headed by a king of arms, the highest ranking officer of arms. "Pursuivants" (literally "followers") were apprentice heralds.

All heralds wore the arms of their master, together with certain other insignia designating their exact rank, and by the 15th century the heralds had assumed a more respectable role than in earlier times.

▲ *Jean le Fevre, King of Arms to the Order of the Golden Fleece, 1431, wearing the tabard of his master, the Duke of Burgundy.*

▲ *John Talbot, Earl of Shrewsbury (1390–1453), is portrayed here wearing his distinctive heraldic tabard.*

▼ *An armorial from the 15th century, showing shields of the knights of Normandy.*

HERALDS AT WAR

On the medieval battlefield, where strategy and tactics took second place to precedence among the nobility, the heralds were attached to the retinue of the marshal who led the army, and assisted him in marshalling the forces on the battlefield, in camp and on the march.

The heralds were given the medieval equivalent of diplomatic immunity, even when journeying in a country at war with their own. They were kept busy on missions of national and royal importance, treating with the opposite side, helping in exchanges of prisoners or the ransom of knights. At such times they would regard each other as members of an international fraternity, often speaking each other's language. This degree of companionship between heralds went so far as keeping council with each other on the field of battle and exchanging tallies of the dead.

An account of a battle between the French and the English in 1453, at Castillon in France, illustrates the nature of medieval warfare and the relationship between herald and master. Among those killed was the English commander John Talbot, Earl of Shrewsbury. So disfigured was the corpse, that Talbot's personal herald could not identify his lord, until, that is, he placed a finger in the bloody maw that was the Earl's mouth, feeling for a gap between his teeth. Upon finding it he took off his tabard, signifying the end of his office, and only then did he sink down and mourn the death of his master.

THE OFFICE OF THE HERALDS

Few countries today still retain any formal heraldic corporate body, but each nation retains its own distinct heraldic styles, laws and customs, reaching back through many centuries. The English College of Arms in London is today the most active, and the longest surviving, heraldic authority, having received its first charter of incorporation in 1484, during the brief reign of Richard III.

THE HOME OF THE COLLEGE OF ARMS

Richard III gave the officers of arms a house called Coldharbour in London, but his successor, Henry VII (1485–1509), promptly gave this building to his mother, Margaret Beaufort. It was not until 1558 that the heralds were once again given a permanent home, this time by Mary Tudor. Although the original building, called Derby House, was destroyed during the Great Fire of London in 1666, the College of Arms has had its home on the same site beside the Thames ever since. Set into the façade of the building are plaques bearing the heraldic devices of the Stanley family, Earls of Derby, who were the original owners of the house destroyed in the Great Fire. The heraldry includes the Stanley badge of an eagle's leg "erased a la quise" (torn away at the thigh).

PRINCIPAL OFFICERS OF ARMS

Since medieval times, officers of arms have been divided into three ranks: kings of arms, heralds and pursuivants. In England, the officer of state responsible for overall control of matters heraldic and ceremonial is the Earl Marshal of England, the Duke of Norfolk, in whose family the office is hereditary.

From at least 1300 (probably earlier) there seems to have been a territorial division of heraldic duties in England. North of the River Trent heraldic matters are controlled by Norroy (or "Northern") King of Arms. South of the Trent, the officer responsible for overseeing grants of arms and other such duties is Clarenceux King of Arms, who most probably takes his title from the private herald of the medieval Dukes of Clarence.

In 1415 William Bruges was the first officer appointed as "Garter King of Arms". Two years later he was given further precedence as the principal king of arms, a fact that was to rankle with the regional kings of arms who wished to lose none of their own powers. Among the duties of Garter is the overseeing of all patents of arms, heraldic matters concerning the Order of the Garter itself (the most senior order of knighthood in Britain, whence comes his title), and the introduction of new peers into the House of Lords.

THE MODERN ENGLISH HERALD

Like their late medieval forebears, heralds today are concerned on a daily basis with the granting of arms, both to individuals and to corporate bodies. They are also often consulted for their expertise in historical matters, from pedigrees to providing background material for television documentaries or films. More formally, they act as assistants and advisors to the Earl Marshal at great state occasions such

▶ *An English king of arms of 1805, depicted wearing his crown of office.*

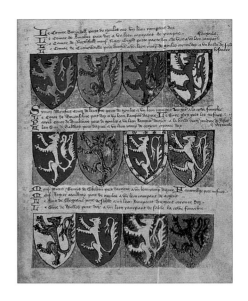

▲ *A page of an ordinary of arms – a list of charges used in heraldry – shows lions rampant and their combinations in family arms.*

as the coronation of the sovereign, or the state opening of Parliament. In addition to the officers employed on a full time, or "ordinary", basis, there are others who, through their own merit, are singled out by the Earl Marshal to be "extraordinary" pursuivants or heralds. They are honorary heralds who exercise ceremonial duties on an occasional basis. The extraordinary officers hold titles taken from the various peerages held by the Earl Marshal.

The English College of Arms is the largest heraldic authority and makes about 200 grants of arms each year. Other nations with heraldic authorities include Scotland, Ireland, South Africa and Canada.

THE ENGLISH HERALDS

Garter King of Arms The principal herald, whose title comes from his duties to the Order of the Garter.

Clarenceux The title probably originated with the herald of the Duke of Clarence, third son of Edward III; responsible for matters south of the River Trent.

Norroy and Ulster "Northern King", responsible for affairs north of the River Trent; his office was twinned with Ulster in 1943.

HERALDS:

All the heralds are named after possessions of the royal family, or, in the case of Somerset, the Beaufort family.

Chester   **Lancaster**   **Richmond**   **Somerset**   **Windsor**   **York**

PURSUIVANTS:

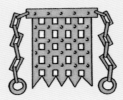

Bluemantle Named after the blue field of the arms of France.

Portcullis Named after the badge of the Tudors/Beauforts.

Rouge Croix Named after the red cross of St George.

Rouge Dragon Named after the supporters of the Tudor arms.

EXTRAORDINARIES:

Beaumont Pursuivant   **Maltravers Pursuivant**   **Surrey Pursuivant**   **Howard Pursuivant**   **Wales Herald Extraordinary**

TABARDS AND INSIGNIA

At one time all herals wore some form of official dress, but in most nations this custom came to an end after World War I. Now, only English and Scottish officers of arms maintain their ceremonial garb. On British state occasions, such as the coronation of a sovereign, the officers of arms will wear their full heraldic regalia of tabard and knee breeches, and carry their wands or staves of office, thereby continuing a tradition unbroken for seven centuries and more.

THE TABARD

In the 13th century, when the herald acted as his master's messenger or "envoy", he would probably have worn the latter's own tabard, or short surcoat, and this would most likely have been a cast-off garment that had lost its first bloom. The tabard of the time would have been constructed from several layers of cloth cut in the form of a thick letter "T". The front and back

▶ *Gentil Oiseau Pursuivant of the Holy Roman Empire, c1450, tabard athwart.*

▼ *Imperial heralds in the funeral procession of Spain's Charles V, 1558.*

panels and both the sleeves were embroidered with the arms of the master. A pursuivant was singled out from officers of arms of higher rank by wearing his tabard "athwart": the shorter panels designed to fit over the arms were worn over the chest and back, with the longer panels over the arms. In England this practice was known from the 15th until the late 17th century, and it was customary for the tabard to be arranged in this way by the Earl Marshal when the pursuivant was admitted to the office. If the pursuivant was later promoted to the rank of herald, the tabard was turned around to its more normal position.

On certain occasions, heralds would wear the tabard of a lord other than their own, particularly during funerals of the major nobility, when they would

◀ *The tabard of John Anstis the Elder, who was the English Garter King of Arms from 1718 to 1744.*

wear tabards bearing the arms of the deceased. They might also have their tabards decorated with shields of other lords, knights and judges present at a tournament. This is splendidly illustrated in one of the great heraldic works of art, *Le Livre des Tournois (The Book of Tourneys)* by King René of Anjou (1409–80). He founded the Order of the Crescent in 1448 and, in between organizing countless tournaments, wrote the work in 1450 and helped to illustrate its pages.

From the 16th century onwards it would seem that officers of arms of different degrees – king of arms, herald and pursuivant – each wore a tabard made from materials commensurate with their

▲ *Russian heralds at the forefront of the procession at the coronation of Nicholas II of Russia in 1896.*

TABARDS AND INSIGNIA **37**

rank; in France, each rank's garments were distinguished by name. The practice is still maintained in England and Scotland, where kings of arms wear velvet, heralds have satin, and pursuivants silk damask tabards. Each tabard is heavy and the wearer has to be dressed by experts for ceremonial events.

A story is told of a recent state occasion when it was arranged that the English officers of arms should sit together in a row. As space was limited, they were packed together very tightly, with unfortunate results: the gold wires on the English royal lion and the harp of Ireland became knitted together, and after the ceremony the row of royal officers had to be prized apart.

◄ *King Edward VIII of England and his officers of arms in full regalia, at the State Opening of Parliament in 1936.*

CROWNS AND SCEPTRES

Kings of arms are known to have worn crowns from the 15th century, when they seem to have been set with little shields and lozenges. The English kings of arms today still include in their insignia crowns designed in the early 18th century bearing a standing circle of stylized leaves.

Officers of arms from various nations have long worn badges of office and carried sceptres or wands, which usually differ in detail according to rank. Garter King of Arms has a badge and sceptre for his office, both of which bear the arms of the Order of the Garter, while the sceptre also bears the royal arms.

In 1906 the English regional kings of arms, heralds and pursuivants were given black batons with gilt ends, each with the badge of their particular office attached at the head. These were replaced in 1953 with white ones based on earlier models, the heads of which were said to bear blue birds or martlets. The current rods still have a blue bird, which is similar to those birds in the arms of the College of Arms. The form carried by the officers ordinary also has a gold coronet at its head, while that of the officers extraordinary does not.

▼ *The neck badge of an English officer of arms, still in use today.*

▼ *The badge and sceptre of Garter Principal King of Arms.*

▼ *The old-style baton of Clarenceux King of Arms.*

THE RIGHT TO ARMS

Heraldic writers through the ages have concerned themselves over the exact nature of arms – who should bear them, when and why, and whether they indicate noble status. The feudal structure of medieval European society only served to help the heraldic cause – what was good for the local ruler was also good for his vassals. By the 14th century the users of heraldry included not only knights and their overlords, but also their ladies. Other sections of society, such as abbeys and their abbots, and towns and their burghers, were also keen to embrace the noble art.

THE SPREAD OF HERALDRY
The heady combination of colour and symbolism meant that heraldry was soon adopted and adapted to suit the requirements of the nobles of many European nations. On the fringes of Europe, in Russia, Lithuania, Poland and Hungary, the military elite saw the appeal of the new science. In Poland, where the noble tribe, or *ród*, was the essential unit of society, the old tribal symbols were adapted to fit the heraldic shield. Unlike the rest of Europe, one shield of arms was used by the entire tribe, and the distinguishing marks that identify family branches in other countries are virtually unknown in Polish heraldry. The Hungarian nobility went for family arms, and at least a third of these referred to the enduring battle against the Islamic "Turkish menace", which for centuries attempted to make inroads into the eastern borders of Christendom. Disembodied parts of dead Turks featured on many Hungarian shields.

Heraldry's pictorial nature made it an ideal medium for the decoration of houses, castles, cathedrals and town halls, on the grand or miniature scale. It could dignify the heading of an illuminated address, supply the design for a signet ring, or decorate

▲ *A Hungarian grant of arms from the early 16th century, showing the age-old fight between the Hungarians and the Turks.*

▶ *A page of a pedigree, with "tricked" arms of the Lambert family, from the herald's visitation notes of Wiltshire, 1565.*

▼ *A Flemish armorial pedigree, c1590, of the Despres family.*

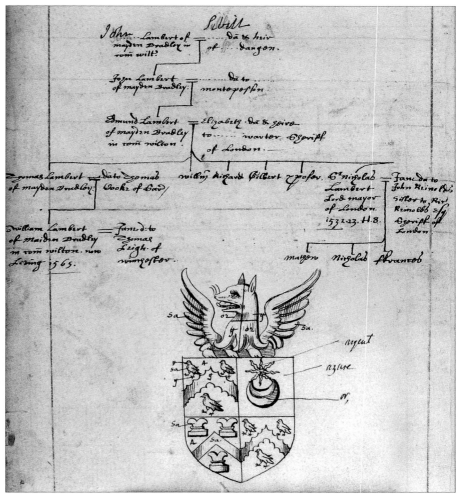

▲ *Christine de Pisan presents her famous and extensive works on chivalry to King Charles VI of France.*

the elaborate wedding arches erected by a loyal populace to welcome a princely bride and groom: all were excellent stages for the display of armorial bearings.

The desire to be identified by arms filtered down through the classes so that many a new-made man, with the power of money behind him, attempted to gain both shield and crest for himself and his heirs, and there were always purveyors of arms who were pleased to oblige with a suitable design: no matter that it was not lawfully gained, it looked good. To counteract the inroads that merchants and other self-made men were making into their prerogatives, the nobility looked to their pedigrees – their authentic arms provided proof of their noble descent and guaranteed their right to acceptance at court and to the ancient orders of chivalry.

THE REGULATION OF HERALDRY

In her book *Le Livre des Faits d'Armes et de Chevalerie*, Christine de Pisan describes a supposed discourse with her spiritual advisor, the Abbé Honoré Bonet, a famed writer on chivalry who had died many years before. Among the questions posed by Christine are, "If a man adopts arms already borne by another, may he retain them?" to which the answer is, "No". Another question is, "If a German knight entering the realm of France finds a Frenchman using the same arms, has the German a just cause for complaint?" Again the answer from Bonet is "No", as they are subjects of different countries and princes.

Which individuals and institutions are, or were, entitled to bear arms? The answer is not simple and depends very much on the age and the nation involved. In some countries, arms have been held only by the nobility. In France during the 17th century, however, even peasants were encouraged to bear a shield of arms, so that they could be taxed for it. In many countries, personal arms can now be adopted at will and may, as in Sweden, be lumped together legally with trademarks and afforded the same protection. Stronger protection tends to be given to civic and military heraldry.

England and Scotland have stringent and longstanding measures in place to protect arms, and during the reign of Henry VIII the English heralds were empowered by royal command to go into the shires and seek out false gentlemen who had assumed arms without due cause. These heraldic progresses were known as "visitations". In the Holy Roman Empire the right to grant arms was at times delegated to the *Hofpfalzgrafen* or "counts of the palace".

THE COURT OF CHIVALRY

In England and Wales the basis of the law of arms is that no one may bear and use them without lawful authority, and that arms are an inalienable right, inherited in accordance with the laws and usages of arms. If, in the view of an officer of arms, these laws are being infringed, the offended party has the right to take the case to the Court of Chivalry, which last sat in 1954 to hear a case brought by the Lord Mayor, aldermen and the citizens of Manchester against the Manchester Palace of Varieties Ltd. The plaintiffs had alleged that the defendants had made illegal use of the arms of the Corporation of Manchester on their company seal. The case was judged in favour of the plaintiffs.

The English Court of Chivalry has its origins in the Courts of the Constable and Marshal, and dates from the first half of the 14th century. As matters armorial were associated with the military class, the chief of the army sits in judgement.

▼ *The Court of Chivalry in session at the College of Arms, London, 1800.*

THE HERALDIC FUNERAL

People of wealth and station in society required a good send-off, commensurate with their rank. The art of "dying well" was much on the minds of the late medieval nobility of Europe, but in the main this meant shows of largesse to the poor and payments for masses to be sung to propel the soul heavenwards. However, just so that God and the angels would know exactly who they were dealing with, the trappings of rank were displayed prominently during the lying-in-state, at the funeral and at the place of burial.

By the 14th century it had become the practice at funerals of royalty and the nobility for a prominent display of heraldry to be included in the pageantry of the event, and these heraldic funerals became increasingly elaborate statements of the deceased's social status and wealth.

THE FUNERAL TRAPPINGS

During the procession the coffin would probably be covered by a pall bearing the arms of the deceased. For members of high nobility and royalty the bier might also be surmounted by a faithful representation of the dead person, dressed in robes of degree

▼ The design of 1619 for the hearse of Anne of Denmark, Queen of James I.

and coronet. On either side of the bier would walk heralds bearing the elements of the deceased's heraldic achievement – his helm and crest, shield of arms, tabard, gauntlets, spurs and sword.

Central to the display in the church was the hearse, a large and often elaborate temporary structure made of wood, metal and cloth, built in the main body of the church. For higher ranks, the hearse was sometimes so elaborate it resembled the chapel in which the deceased would in due course be buried. The hearse had receptacles for burning tapers, in between which would be set the armorial bearings of the deceased, usually made of buckram.

Upon entering the church the coffin would be placed within the rails of the hearse, where the principal mourners would also take their places. The funeral of a high-ranking member of the nobility was attended not only by family members and other mourners, but even by the deceased's warhorse, decked out in the heraldic trappings of its master.

In Italy and Spain, well into the 20th century, the high-born would have lain "in state" at home before the funeral. The body lay either in a coffin or on a bed of state, dressed in court dress, with the bed itself covered with cloth of gold upon which

▲ The "State Ship" of Charles V, Holy Roman Emperor, 1558: part of the spectacle of the royal funeral in Renaissance Europe.

were embroidered the family arms. For the highest rank, household staff would hold mourning banners bearing arms. The hearse was also decorated by a number of

▼ The tomb of the Black Prince, in Canterbury Cathedral, England, displays his full regalia to show his knightly rank.

banners, standards, guidons and lesser flags, the exact number of which was regulated by degree. These and the rest of the achievement would in time be hung near to the burial place of the deceased, providing an awesome display of pomp.

THE HERALDS' ROLE

In Britain, the great age of the heraldic funeral was between 1500 and 1700. The marshalling of such events was largely the responsibility of the officers of arms, who jealously guarded their rights because of the fees due to them, which were known as "funeral droits". These were payable from the estate of the deceased and were considerable, the fee itself depending on the deceased's degree and the rank of the herald. The English heralds kept a keen eye on anyone – especially painters and engravers – who might encroach on their offices, and at times the various parties set to brawling with each other over their fees at the very door of the church, as the noble corpse was going to its final rest.

Every facet of the noble funeral was regulated by the heralds, from the number of mourners, their degree and the size of their trains, to the number, shape and size of the flags. The following letter to Garter Dethick, who held office from 1586–1606, gives some idea of the detail involved:

Good Mr Garter, I pray you, as your leisure doth best serve you, set down advisedly and exactly, in every particular itself, the number of mourners due to my calling, being a Viscountess of birth, with the number of waiting-women for myself, and the women mourners, which, with the chief mourner and her that shall bear the trayne, will be in number ten, beside waiting women, pages and gentlemen wishers. Then I pray you the number of chief mourners of Lords, Knights and gentlemen... Good Mr Garter, do it exactly; for I find forewarnings that bid me to provide a pick-axe etc. So with my most friendly commendation to you, I rest,

Your old Mistress and Friend,
Elizabeth Russel, Dowager.

▲ *The coffin of Christine, Duchess of Braunschweig-Bevern; the arms are those of her mother's family, Pfalz-Zweibrucken.*

The reply Mr Garter sent is very lengthy and includes the following details for the funeral procession:

That it include 4 Bannerolls [a type of heraldic banner showing "impalements" for family marriages], the Great Banner borne by a Knight or esquire, a preacher, a Garter King of Arms and 2 heralds. The Lady Chief Mourner was

▲ *The heraldic fittings on the coffin of the widowed Countess of Cholmondeley, 18th century, in Malpas Church, Cheshire, England.*

to have for her gown, mantle, traynes, hood and tippets, 11 yards of black cloth. Garter King of Arms was allowed liveries as a knight, 6 yards of cloth, the heralds 5 yards...

▼ *The heraldic achievements – including the shield, sword, helmet and crest – being carried by mourning attendants at the funeral of Charles VI of France, 1422.*

THE ROTHES FUNERAL

The funeral of John, 1st and only Duke of Rothes, shows just what a heraldic funeral on the grand scale involved. The Duke had died on 27 July 1681, and his funeral took place almost a month later on 23 August. Having held the office of Lord High Chancellor of Scotland, he was afforded a full state funeral. It included every possible type of heraldic funeral trapping, as well as two complete regiments of artillery.

After the troops there followed the two conductors with crêpe in their hats and black staves over their shoulders, then two little "gumpheons" (gonfalones or square flags), one bearing a death's head with the

◄ The monument to Alice, Dowager Countess of Derby (d1636–7) is thought to be a representation of a heraldic hearse.

words *Memento mori* ("Remember you must die"), the other bearing an hourglass with the words *Fugit hora* ("Hours fly"). Then there followed a line of poor men in mourning cloaks that bore the Duke's cipher and coronet. Next came a trumpeter, his banner charged with the ducal achievement, then a cavalier on horseback. Next was a banner of the ducal colours or liveries borne by a gentleman. He was followed by the Duke's servants.

There then followed the Pencil of Honour, a swallow-tailed flag bearing the entire achievement, then one with the paternal arms (Leslie), followed by the Standard of Honour (similar to the pencil but with a square end). The warhorse was led by two "lacquies", who were bareheaded. Two trumpeters followed, then the Bute and Carrick pursuivants of arms in mourning gowns and tabards. Another small group of heraldic flags then followed: the Great Gumpheon, another gumpheon bearing the arms of Abernethy with a "laurel wreath in mourning" and the Little Mourning Standard.

After a group of gentlemen in mourning gowns and hats, there followed another two pursuivants, Kintyre and Dingwall, after which came the spurs, gauntlets, the breastplate, targe (shield), helm and wreath, and sword. Two more retainers then led the deceased's packhorse, after

which walked a goodly procession of officers and counsellors of Edinburgh, members of the judiciary and government and representatives of the peerage, followed by the last of the pursuivants, Unicorn and Ormonde. Two trumpeters then announced eight bearers with banners of kinship. On the paternal side (the right) were those of the Earl of Roxburgh, Hamilton of Evandale, the Earl of Perth and the Earl of Rothes; and on the left the descent through his mother from the Duke of Antragne, the Earl of Tullibardine, the Duke of Lennox and the Earl of Mar.

The mourning horse then followed, bearing a black trapper adorned with panels bearing the ducal arms. The last of the heraldic flags, the Great Mourning Banner, bore the ducal achievement and motto. Two more trumpeters announced six heralds: Islay, with the shield of Leslie; Albany, with that of Abernethy; Marchmont, with the crest, motto and wreath; Rothesay with the helm, coronet and mantling; Snowdon with the sword and Ross with the targe.

The Duke's servants and household officers followed, after which was led the Duke's horse for riding to Parliament covered with a richly embroidered saddlecloth. Next came a gentleman bearing the Duke's coronet (with cap), followed by two archbishops and then Lord Lyon (the principal Scottish officer of arms) in tabard and

▼ The funeral of Elizabeth I of England in 1603. The mourners carry banners of the Queen's ancestors.

mourning cloak carrying a diamond-shaped "hatchment" bearing the Duke's entire heraldic achievement.

More trappings of Parliament followed, including the Lord Chancellor's purse. Then followed the most extraordinary sight of the whole incredible spectacle: the coffin of the Duke itself, carried beneath a pall or mortcloth decorated with the arms of the Duke and his relations. These were interspersed with death's heads, ciphers and silver tears. Upon the cloth, which was borne along by close relations, was the Duke's coronet. The coffin was carried beneath a great canopy decorated like the pall, the poles of which were carried by noblemen's sons. Then followed the principal mourners and the mourning coach, the official procession being brought to a close by His Majesty's Guard.

The procession was said to have reached 8km (5 miles) in length. The entire affair cost about £30,000 ($42,000), the equivalent of some £3 ($4.2) million at today's prices, which was supposed to have been paid by the government, although in the end the family was left to pick up most of the enormous bill.

From the end of the 17th century, Protestant Britain saw a "noble rebellion" against the profligate cost of the grand heraldic funeral, which had become prohibitive even for the richest of families. Many of the traditions and the trappings that had been associated with such a funeral, such as armour for example, had themselves become long outdated and scarce, although up to that time there were still specialist manufacturers who carried on producing special "funeral armour".

▲ *The heraldic funeral par excellence: the coffin of the Duke of Rothes is covered with a pall and canopy charged with his arms and teardrops. Note his coronet on the coffin.*

▼ *This small section of the funeral procession of the Duke of Rothes includes his "cavalier" or champion and various types of mourning flags befitting a duke's degree.*

HATCHMENTS AND TRAPPINGS

From the medieval period until quite recently, the death of a member of the nobility was marked by a series of "memorials". While some were temporary, others were permanent, and were principally aimed at maintaining the status quo – the chief weapon in the armoury of status being heraldry.

TOMBS AND HERALDRY

On early memorials, whether in stone and brass, enamelled or carved, heraldry was limited to the bearer's own personal shield and crest. Soon, however, the place of burial was being used as a platform on which the nobility could show off not only the arms of their own family, but also those to whom they were united through marriage. By the Renaissance the grand monuments of the aristocracy displayed a series of shields for family marriages, often borne by fantastical figures such as angels. The children of the deceased were also often depicted on the tombs, kneeling with shields (for boys) and lozenges (for girls). The canopies and sides of the tombs, the dress of the effigies and even the most intricate of decoration might be used to support a display of heraldry. Death itself could be called upon to support the shield, or sometimes the shield of the deceased might be shown upside-down.

In Italy, gravestones often bear fully coloured arms of the deceased executed in *pietra dura*, an inlaying technique using a variety of coloured stones, but in most countries they tend to be carved in local stone and uncoloured. Whereas in Britain the flat stones set into the floors of many parish churches bear the arms of the deceased only, in Germany and the Low Countries they often bear a series of shields down the sides of the stone, those on the left for the father's side, those on the right for the mother's side.

CABINETS D'ARMES

During the Middle Ages, the trappings of knighthood were carried in the funeral procession and afterwards lay in the church near the grave of the deceased. In the Low Countries a new practice grew up in the 16th century, whereby the actual pieces of armour, sword, gauntlets, helm and tabard were replaced with painted reproductions, usually made of wood. These were grouped in a frame, together with the shields of the paternal and maternal grandparents. The background to the display was painted in mourning black. Such framed displays were called *cabinets d'armes*, or *cabinets d'honor*. It is thought that this practice led to the use of hatchments (a corruption of "achievement"), the

▲ *A good example of a cabinet d'armes for a member of the de Schietere family of Bruges who died in 1637.*

diamond-shaped mourning boards, many of which are still found hanging in parish churches in England today. The hatchment was hung outside the home of the deceased for a period of mourning, perhaps as much as a year and a day, indicating to visitors that a death had occurred in the family. The custom still persists in Britain, albeit rarely.

▲ *The hatchment for Prince Leopold, Duke of Albany, youngest son of Queen Victoria.*

▲ *A splendidly restored Totenschild for Bürgermeister Hans Jörg, portrait included.*

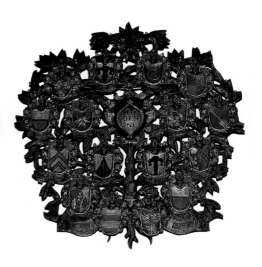

▲ *A Swedish heraldic mourning panel for Per Brahe, d1680.*

DECIPHERING HATCHMENTS

From the background of the hatchment and the composition of the arms, it is possible to work out the sex and marital status of the deceased. For a single person (bachelor, spinster, widow or widower) the background is all black. Where no marriage has existed, a shield (for a man) or a lozenge (for a woman) bearing the patrimonial arms is shown. In the case of a bachelor the helm and crest also appear. As the diamond-shaped lozenge is thought a somewhat plain shape, it is sometimes accompanied by a decorative blue bow.

Things become more complicated when a marriage has been made. When one of the couple survives, the background of the hatchment is divided vertically black and white, with black – as the colour of mourning – behind the deceased's half of the arms and white behind the survivor's half. When a wife dies before her husband, her hatchment bears a shield with no crest (a bow often being substituted), and the right-hand half of the background is black. If the husband dies first the whole achievement is shown, with black behind the left half. If the hatchment is for a widower, an all-black background is shown with shield, crest and marital coat of arms. If it is for a widow, the marital coat appears on a lozenge. These are the simplest cases, and there are many hatchments whose composition taxes the onlooker and can prove hard to interpret: in the case of a man who has married several times, for instance, the arms of all his wives may appear, with separate backing for each marriage.

Although a family motto often appears on a man's hatchment, it is just as likely to be replaced by a Latin phrase relating to death and resurrection, such as *Resurgam* ("I shall rise again"), *In coelo quis* ("There is rest in heaven") or *Mors janua vitae* ("Death is the doorway to life").

While many English parish churches contain one or two hatchments to a lord of the manor, or previous vicar, some have splendid collections for a whole family: such as that of the Hulse family of Breamore, Hampshire, where the church displays a set of hatchments that date from the early 18th century to the 1990s.

HATCHMENT DESIGNS

Examples of designs on funeral hatchments, which declare the status and position of the deceased person. From top – left to right – these are hatchments for: 1) A married man, 2) a married woman (note the bow on the top), 3) a widowed man, 4) an unmarried man, 5) a widowed woman, 6) an unmarried woman, 7–10) a widowed man who has survived two wives.

THE COAT
OF ARMS

The phrase "coat of arms" is a variant of the more ancient term "coat armour", which describes one of heraldry's principal accoutrements, the surcoat or tabard, which was worn for much of the late medieval period over a warrior's armour. Coat of arms is therefore something of a misnomer, for while it originally meant an actual garment bearing armorial devices, it has now come to represent the entire panoply of the personal achievement of arms, including shield, helm, crest, mantling, motto and supporters – but without any sign of an actual coat. The style of the full achievement of arms has changed over the centuries, developing from simple representations to the florid artistic visions of the Rococo period and the absurdities of the 19th century, when a crest might not connect to its helmet, and mantling looked more like foliage than cloth. An important factor to remember when describing a coat of arms is that the shield is described from the bearer's position behind it. The heraldic right, called dexter, and the heraldic left, called sinister, are the opposite to the normal right and left.

◄ *The arms and proud motto of the Spanish family,*
Manrique de Lara.

THE COMPLETE ACHIEVEMENT

The heraldic achievement is a grand affair consisting of several component parts. The first is the arms themselves on the shield, surmounted by the helmet, the detail of which may change to denote the rank or degree of the armiger. On the helmet usually sits that other important heraldic accoutrement, the crest. Hanging from the top of the helmet is a loose piece of cloth known as the mantling. For the medieval knight this cloth once perhaps served to give some protection to the back of the helmet; in heraldry it is normally depicted in the main metal and colour of the arms.

The mantling is attached to the helmet by means of twists of cord known as the wreath or torse. As with the mantling, the twists tend to be in the principal tinctures of the arms. If a crest coronet or circlet is

▶ *A full achievement typical of those granted in modern times by the English College of Arms, in this case to the author.*

▼ *The same achievement as right, but this black and white depiction of it has been hatched – each colour is represented by a system of lines and dots.*

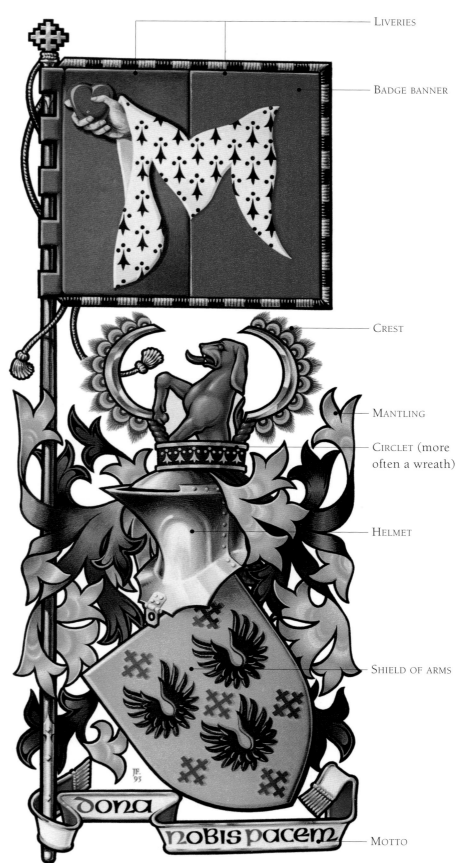

LIVERIES

BADGE BANNER

CREST

MANTLING

CIRCLET (more often a wreath)

HELMET

SHIELD OF ARMS

MOTTO

DONA NOBIS PACEM

dona nobis pacem

PAVILION OR MANTLE

CROWN OR CORONET

WREATH

CREST

BADGE BANNER

SUPPORTERS

SHIELD OF ARMS

COMPARTMENT

DECORATIONS

▲ *The more elaborate full achievement of nobility, in this case the emperors of Germany, with crown and supporters.*

achievement of any armiger. For those of higher rank the full achievement can be much grander, with the shield supported by men or beasts; if the holder has a title, such as count or duke, the coronet of rank will also appear. In Britain the coronet sits above the shield, between it and the helm. In other nations the coronet might appear on the helm.

If the armiger is a member of an order of knighthood, the circlet or collar of his order may encircle the shield. For titled members of the aristocracy, a robe or mantle might also appear as a backdrop to the arms. Sovereigns tend to replace the mantle with the pavilion – a domed cloth on which sits the crown.

Such an achievement is a complex and expensive composition to show in its entirety, so an armiger is more likely to denote ownership of property, whether on a book cover or a private jet, by using just the crest or the combination or crest and motto. Holders of a peerage might also place their coronet above the crest or simple shield of arms. Once arms have been granted they may be displayed at will.

borne this usually replaces the wreath (as in the author's arms shown left) although sometimes the two items do appear one on top of the other. In English heraldry a motto, if borne, appears below the shield; in Scotland, above it. If a badge is also borne by the armiger it might appear alongside the full achievement on a banner of the liveries, as seen here, but this is not common.

This combination – of shield of arms, helm, crest, mantling and wreath – is the

▶ *The arms of Queen Elizabeth II: the shield is surmounted by the gold helmet of a sovereign.*

THE SHIELD

Ever since its inception, heraldry has relied on the shield for the main display of armorial bearings. All other parts of the achievement – such as the crest, mantling, wreath and supporters – depend on the shield, and while there are many cases of a shield of arms being granted by itself, no one can be granted a crest unless the family has at some time previously been granted a shield of arms. Although armorial bearings are often found on different items such as banners and surcoats, it is the shield that is considered the armorial platform without equal.

EARLY SHIELDS

From the very beginnings of organized fighting, the shield was one of the principal means of protection, and was used to stop sword, axe or arrow. Once a weapon passed that first defence, the only things left to protect the soldier were his body armour and his own fighting skills.

The ancient Greeks used round shields, while the Romans preferred large rectangular shields with slightly rounded ends. Each nation's soldiers decorated their shields with various devices: these might be national, regimental or tribal in nature, but were not truly heraldic in that they

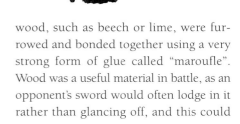

▶ *A rare medieval battle shield, an ideal platform for the heraldry that followed in the 13th and 14th centuries.*

were seldom personal, nor did they have any hereditary significance.

SHIELD CONSTRUCTION

At the start of the heraldic story in the second half of the 12th century, the shield was so long that it could cover almost half the bearer's body, and it was normally curved to fit around the torso. The shields used at the Battle of Hastings were kite-shaped and this style continued into the early 1200s, although by then the top edge of the shield was usually straight. Gradually, as the wearing of plate armour increased, the shield diminished in size until it was about a third of the height of the bearer.

Surviving medieval shields show that they were usually made of wooden sheets glued together in an early form of plywood. Several sheets of coarse-grained wood, such as beech or lime, were furrowed and bonded together using a very strong form of glue called "maroufle". Wood was a useful material in battle, as an opponent's sword would often lodge in it rather than glancing off, and this could

▼ *Round shields favoured by Greek warriors often showed devices that many centuries later appeared in heraldry.*

▼ *The seal of Count Conrad of Oettingen, c1229, shows heraldic charges almost certainly arising from the shield's construction.*

▼ *The English army at Hastings carried long kite-shaped shields, the shape adapted to heraldic usage a century later.*

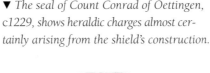

▲ *Examples of heraldic devices that most probably arose from the construction of the medieval shield. Clockwise from top left, the shields are those of Valletort, Navarre, Mandeville and Holstein.*

give the shield-bearer a split-second advantage, which could make the difference between life and death. The shield was covered with leather (from horse, ass or buck), parchment or linen. The leather was first boiled in oil to make cuir-bouilli, another good defensive material. Often the exterior was also coated with gesso, or fine plaster, into which a decorative "diapered" pattern might be worked, resembling the designs woven into damask fabrics. Over the gesso surface the armorial bearings of the wearer were applied. These could either be painted flush with the surface, or moulded into slight relief.

SHIELD FITTINGS

The shield was given extra strength by nailing on metal studs, bands and other reinforcements, and some of these additions probably gave rise to heraldic charges themselves. Within this class of "structural" heraldry are examples such as the arms of the great Anglo-Norman family of Mandeville, whose "escarbuncle" (a wheel-like device in the centre of the shield) probably started off as a metal boss. The arms of Count Conrad II of Oettingen (*c*1229) show a "saltire" or diagonal cross, which probably originated as metal reinforcing bands, and those of Reginald de

Valletourt of Cornwall, from the time of King John, probably show not only the wooden slattings of the shield but the strengthening edge with its nails. It is also possible that the chain in the arms of Navarre started in similar fashion. Even the nettleleaf of Holstein was probably formed by a serrated metal border.

Various materials, from leather to padded cloth, were used for the inner side of the shield, and to these were fixed straps and padded cushions, the latter to allow extra comfort for the bearer and also to absorb the shock of sword and axe blows. Most medieval shields were also contoured to fit the body. Obviously the shield could not be held at all times; when not actually in use it was strung around the bearer's side by a leather strap known as a "guige".

All of this shows a sensible approach to the business of war as seen from the bearer's point of view. The medieval armourer was highly skilled and his shield, despite its size, was surprisingly light and well constructed, as was late medieval armour in general. The most important collection of surviving medieval shields is now in the University Museum of Marburg in Hesse, Germany. They originally lay in

▲ *The German and Italian knights in this 14th-century battle scene bear the flatiron or heater-shaped shield, which became the most common platform for heraldry.*

the Elisabethkirche in Marburg, having been placed there by members of the Teutonic Order, and it is from them that historians have learned much about the construction of the shield.

By the late 13th century the shield's size had diminished considerably, and it had taken the form of the "heater" shield, so-called because it was shaped like the base of a flatiron. The heater shield proved remarkably popular and it is this shape that in the main has served heraldry since the 14th century.

THE TOURNEY SHIELD

From the late 14th century a new form of shield appeared, specifically for use on the tourney field. It was in the shape of a rectangle with curved edges – usually with slightly concave sides and top and with a convex base. While the war shield retained its flatiron shape for centuries, for tournaments the shield became a much more decorated affair, with scalloped edges and

► *The simple heater shield of the late 13th century.*

▲ *As art forms developed more elaborate and florid designs so too did the heraldic shield, although in this example the notch at the top for the lance does still survive.*

▲ *Knights taking part in a tournament of the 15th century bear concave shields specially designed for the tilt.*

flutings. The tourney shield often bore elaborate devices – sometimes they were partially heraldic, often not – which gave out bold messages of love and bravura, the former for the ladies sitting in the viewing galleries around the arena, the latter for any would-be challenger. For use in jousting,

the shield might also have a special notch cut out of the top corner to allow the lance to be "couched", or rested, more easily. By the late 15th century the armourer's expertise had advanced to such a degree that special rivets and bolts were often fitted on the body plates to take lance-rests and extra defences. There was at one time a tourney shield that could actually be fixed to the wearer's breastplate, and the lance rested at its corner.

THE SHIELD IN HERALDRY
Strictly, for the purposes of heraldry, the shield takes one of two forms. The first is the shield proper, which bears the arms of men, and the second is the lozenge, a diamond-shaped device used to display the arms of women. In fact, however, the shape of the heraldic shield varied considerably over the centuries and can reveal much about the period when it was used, and even the country of origin of the bearer. The tourney shield made its appearance in heraldry and, along with the heater shield, was often depicted as being tilted slightly to one side. There is nothing heraldically significant in this: along with

▼ *From the Renaissance the mantling and helm became ever more intricate, as in this example from the mid-16th century.*

all the fancifully shaped shields that appeared on paper and in architecture, it simply reflected the artistic style of the period in which it was used.

FASHIONS IN HERALDIC ART
From the 12th to the 16th century, the shapes of heraldic shields followed the fashions of real shields used in battle, but after the Renaissance artistic licence made inroads into all manner of decorations –

◄ *This monument to the Earl of Hereford from 1621 shows how the shield itself began to assume a non-martial appearance.*

including heraldry. Artists and engravers saw the shield, and the armorial accoutrements that surrounded it, as ideal objects for embellishment. The arms were placed in highly ornate frames, held up by cherubs and draped with garlands, until in many cases the actual arms appear as an afterthought in the decorative scheme. But the Renaissance treatment of heraldry was nothing compared with the Rococo style of the 18th century, when shields ceased to be anything of the sort, instead becoming swirling and curving creations resembling the inside of a seashell. The heraldic shield took on forms that a medieval knight would have gaped at – certainly the scroll-like edges and fantastical flutings would have caused more harm than good if he had borne such a shield on the battlefield, as the enemy's lance could have found plenty of handy points to

▼ *The climax of heraldic design was the fantastical Rococo period, when the arms became simply an excuse for the frame.*

affix to, rather than being deflected by the clean curves of the medieval shield.

The Rococo style had emerged from a great period of artistic and architectural triumph – the Baroque. No visitor to Rome can fail to be impressed at the sheer size of heraldic decoration lavished on the city by the popes of that period, each one seemingly wanting to outdo his predecessor by placing his own arms over gateways and triumphal arches, and on obelisks. The supreme example of heraldic ostentation must be the design of the church of Sant'Ivo alla Sapienza in Rome. Because Pope Urban VIII (1623–44) was a member of the Barberini family, the architect, Francesco Borromini, is said to have based his plan on the heraldic bees that appeared in the Barberini arms.

◀ *An 18th-century bookplate showing the elaborate heraldic style of the Rococo period.*

COMPLEXITY AND OBFUSCATION

At least the Rococo had some style about it, even if heraldry was corrupted to suit the contorted shapes of that style. What followed in the late 18th and 19th centuries can only be described as the heraldic doldrums. Shields became fat and unattractive, with tiny helmets perched above them bearing outsized crests and even more outsized wreaths, though each dropped well away from the top of the helmet upon which they were meant to sit. Perhaps the shields needed to be fat, given the complexity of designs they had to bear, which sometimes amounted to entire landscapes or complete historical accounts.

▲ *The distinctive horse-head shield and the teardrop form are both shapes that are particularly favoured in Italy as a background for heraldry.*

SHIELD SHAPES
These illustrations show how the heraldic shield developed from the traditional flatiron shape through the tourney shield with the notch, the complexities of the Renaissance and the Rococo, back to the simple designs of modern heraldry and the lozenge for a woman.

Late 12th, early 13th century

Late 13th, early 14th century

15th century

15th century

15th century

Mid-16th century

Late 17th century

Late 17th century

19th century

Lozenge for women

THE CREST

After the shield, the second most important constituent part of an achievement of arms is the crest. This is the three-dimensional object that adorns the top of the helmet. While many modern writers cite the shield on the tomb plate of Geoffrey, Count of Anjou as the first example of true heraldic arms, they often pass over the little lion that adorns the Count's cap. Possibly this is the forerunner of the heraldic crest, although helmets had long been "crested" with various devices, including the brush-like structures surmounting the helmets of Roman legionaries.

THE HELMET AND DISPLAY

The true "heraldic" crest would seem to have taken shape a century or so after the advent of armorial bearings. Manuscripts from the 13th century sometimes show heraldic charges painted on the sides of knights' helmets, and it has been suggested

▼ *The tomb-plate of Geoffrey, Count of Anjou, d1151. His conical cap bears a lion passant – was this in fact an early crest?*

that the paint and lacquer used probably acted as an early form of rustproofing. From the early 13th century the top of the helmet was often flattened out and heightened into a fanlike crest. These projections were ideal for the display of painted motifs, usually copied from the bearer's shield.

Even from this early period the crest would appear to have been associated with men of tournament rank – the higher nobility – and in later centuries in certain countries crests were forbidden to all except those entitled to enter the lists. Tournaments were the most costly of sports and the participants were expected to put on a really exciting display of colour and bravado. Some outstanding examples appear on the seals of German knights from the 13th and 14th centuries. They show crests in the manner of wind chimes or revolving plaques edged in peacock feathers, some of which would whistle and rotate as the bearer charged his opponent, like heraldic mobiles. Such a display – like the wings worn by Polish lancers in the 17th and 18th centuries (which also had whistles attached to them) – was probably intended to strike awe and even terror in the opponent, but also satisfied the vanity of the wearer.

In the 14th century a type of crest called the "panache" was popular, especially among English knights. It consisted of

▼ *These elaborate crests, taken from the personal seals of German knights in the late 14th century and early 15th century, show*

▲ *This crest from a helmet, c1350, is a rare survival of the buffalo horns so beloved by German medieval families.*

layers of feathers decorating the helmet, which rose to a peak, often following the contours of the bascinet – the domed helmet much in vogue at the time.

GERMAN CRESTS

From the 15th century crests became highly complex, and in Germany the craft of crestmaking was a profession of note.

German helmets were often surmounted by buffalo horns or pairs of wings (frequently decorated with charges

wind chimes and mobiles that would have been suitable for a dramatic grand entrance to the tourney field.

▲ *The arms of the Folkunga dynasty of Sweden; the buffalo horns on the helmet are adorned with little flags.*

taken from the shield of arms). It has been suggested that the curved shapes of such ornaments may have aided in the deflection of sword blows. The edges of these typically Germanic crests were further enhanced with little leaves or bells, but the most popular decoration of all was peacock's feathers, which featured on as many as half of all crests.

The spaces between the wings or horns afforded a platform for even greater elaboration: conical caps, towers and human figures were added to elicit the admiration of the tournament audience, and sometimes the crests of two families were combined to make a "crest of alliance". Often the human figures in medieval German crests were without arms, and their dress, or even their skin, forms the mantling of the helm – the material protecting its back and sides. In old German such limbless figures were called *Menschentumpf,* "men's torsos". Unlike German crests, those of the English and French nobility tended

◄ *Menschentumpf (men's torsos) were popular crests in late medieval German heraldry.*

▲ *The Huldenberg Armorial, a Flemish heraldic armorial of the late 15th century, shows the wings and peacock feathers that were popular in north European heraldry.*

to be separate from the mantling. Instead, the crest appeared to sit within a twisted cord of material known as the wreath or torse.

MULTIPLE CRESTS

In Britain, France, Italy and Spain, crests were seldom as complex as those found in Germany, and in those countries a family seldom used more than one crest, as opposed to German aristocracy and royalty, who often had as many as half a dozen or more crested helms above their shields, each crest tending to represent not so much a family as a fiefdom. In Britain, buffalo horn and peacock's feathers are almost unknown, and the heads of men or demicreatures tend to be unaccompanied, unless by crest coronets. In Spanish

heraldry, crests were so rare that they are almost non-existent (only used by a few ancient noble families). Ostrich plumes are the usual adornment to the Spanish heraldic helmet.

Where an English family has assumed a second surname through marriage to a heraldic heiress, a second crest may be adopted. Occasionally, a second crest may be granted or assumed on some special occasion, usually by "augmentation" – an addition to the arms that in some way reflects the gratitude of the donor, who would usually be royal.

▲ *The arms of the Princes of Lippe, late 19th century. In German lands multiple crests were common within the arms of the higher nobility.*

GRUESOME REMINDERS

One of the most deadly creatures in all heraldry must surely be the viper in the crest (and on the shield of arms) of the Visconti family, the medieval rulers of Milan. The various stories of the viper's origin must have bought many a truculent Italian child to obedience. One tale tells of an enormous serpent that had terrorized the locality and had to be placated by regular offerings of fresh babies; it was finally vanquished by an early Visconti. Another story concerns Ottone Visconti, who is said to have killed a Saracen prince, Voluce, beneath the walls of Jerusalem during the First Crusade. Ottone took Voluce's own crest – a ferocious dragon or serpent devouring a child – as his own. No family has enjoyed its heraldry as much as the Visconti, and a special place is afforded to the viper, which has been depicted in the fullest possible way through the centuries, and can be seen today throughout the world on the badge of Alfa-Romeo cars.

Human heads of various races recall past conflicts. Of these, the Saracen's head is the most common, reflecting the exploits of the Crusader knights. The Hazelriggs of Noseley in Leicestershire have as their crest a Scot's head, commemorating the family's part in the harrying of Scotland by Edward III (1327–77). Though they are not used as a crest, it is also worth mentioning the

three Englishmen's heads in the arms of the Welsh family of Bulkeley-Williams. Together with many other Welsh families, they claim descent from the 13th-century Welsh chieftain Edynfed Vychan. The heads commemorate an incident during a conflict between the English and the Welsh, when the chieftain surprised a band of soldiers from the household of Ranulph, Earl of Chester. In the action that followed, three of Ranulph's principal commanders were killed. The story goes that the Tudors, another family who claimed descent from Edynfed Vychan, also adopted the three heads as charges, but upon their arrival at the English court thought it prudent to turn the heads into three helmets.

The Hamond-Graeme baronets (extinct) of the Isle of Wight had – in addition to another – a rather gruesome crest: two erect arms issuing from clouds in the act of removing a human skull from a spike; above the skull a marquess's coronet between two palm branches. The whole composition is a prime example of a "paper crest", which could never actually have adorned a medieval helmet.

The story behind the crest refers to a member of the Graeme family, a follower of the Marquess of Montrose, who was

▼ *The infamous and highly ferocious viper of the Viscontis, devouring a child.*

executed in Edinburgh in 1650 after his attempt to avenge the death of Charles I. The Marquess's head was placed on the roof of the Tolbooth, the city prison, but his Graeme relative managed to retrieve it and hide it until it could be afforded a proper burial in the Montrose vault.

MANTLING AND WREATH

The crested helm was an elaborate affair that was further decorated with a large piece of cloth, secured to the top of the helmet by cords or other fastenings. In

▼ *The rather gruesome crest of the Hamond-Graeme family, in which a skull is lifted from a spike in remembrance of an ancestor's 17th-century exploit.*

▲ *The early heraldry of the Scandinavian nobility closely followed the styles favoured in Germany, as here in the crests of the families of Thott (left) and Wrangel (right)*

of Sweden. The Wrangel crest shows the type of mantling that is reminiscent of its possible origin – a makeshift sunshade used by the Crusaders.

British heraldry this cloth helmet cover is called the mantling. Usually the mantling is bi-coloured – its upper surface bearing the principal colour in the arms and its underside the principal metal – although three or four colours may be employed, as is the case in Spanish and Portuguese heraldry.

In the earliest depiction of crests the cloth mantling was quite simply portrayed, hanging down as one complete piece of cloth covering much of the side of the helmet. Later, especially during the age of heraldic decadence in the 17th and 18th centuries, the mantling was slashed into many elaborate pieces, often resembling foliage rather than cloth. Families of ancient lineage tended to frown on such effete depiction and kept to the simple style of the 14th and 15th centuries.

◄ *An illustration from the Manesse Codex (c1300) in which a certain Herr Harwart fights a bear. The crest above the bear's head is of the early fan-plate type.*

The attachment of mantling and crest to the helm was often hidden by a wreath or torse of twisted cloth, usually in the same colours as the mantling. In Spanish and Portuguese heraldry, the mantling appears not to be connected to the helmet, but is portrayed rather like a backdrop to it. In the late medieval period it was not unknown for the mantling to serve as a setting for charges taken from the arms or family badge.

Various heraldic experts have suggested that both the mantling and the wreath may have originated during the age of the Crusades. Wearing any form of plate armour in the heat of the Middle Eastern sun cannot have been pleasant, and there are tales of knights actually cooking in their kit. It is possible that some degree of comfort may have been gained from adapting the local headdress and wearing it over the top of the helmet, and certainly the combination of simple mantling and wreath bears a strong similarity to traditional Arab headgear.

THE HELM AND CORONET

◄ *The helm show in King René's tournament book – here the crest of a knight who has offended a lady is struck down.*

As early as the 12th century, the mounted warrior's helmet had become a platform for heraldic colour and charges, which were often painted on its side and may have helped to protect its surface.

▼ *Helmets of degree for French royals and nobles in the second half of the 18th century.*

However, in terms of armorial bearings it was a long time before the helmet itself became a truly heraldic accessory – before the late 15th century it was included in the coat of arms simply as a support for the crest. The helmets depicted in early heraldic manuscripts and on monumental effigies followed whatever style happened to be in favour at the time. They were little used to indicate rank, and armorials show all degrees, from knights to monarchs, using the same type of helmet.

HELMETS AND RANK

From around 1500 the bearing of crowns and coronets on the helmets of those of royal rank became common, and at the same time the grilled "pageant helmet" was appearing, which had a number of ornamental bars across the face. During the Renaissance, the depiction of the grills, and even the metals of the helmet, became increasingly embellished according to rank. The helmet was soon to become yet another piece of "paper heraldry", with grandiose patterns, gold and silver edgings and specified numbers of bars depending on the rank of the bearer. The arms of the lesser nobility bore either the closed helm, which had a solid visor and fully covered the face, or the frog-faced tilt helm.

▼ *An Italian ornamental helmet, with crest and wreath from around 1450–70 and other later additions.*

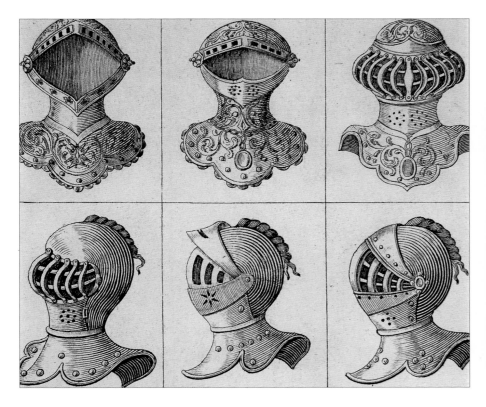

▲ *Heraldic crests were added to whatever style of helmet was popular at the time; here the crest of the Wittelsbach dukes of Bavaria surmounts a sallet helmet.*

▲ *The crowning of Queen Elizabeth II of Great Britain, in 1953, in Westminster Abbey. A coronation is the one occasion when all peers wear their coronets of rank.*

As with most heraldic accoutrements, it was France that led the fashion in the portrayal of helmets. French heralds not only drew up patterns for the helmets of different ranks – from the sovereign (all gold with visor open), down to new nobility (plain steel with three bars) – but also specified the position in which the helmet was to be depicted. Most faced right, or "dexter"; a helmet facing in the opposite direction ("sinister") indicated illegitimacy. Spain and Portugal followed suit with

▲ *A modern heraldic coronet, for a region of the Gabon – l'Ogooué-Ivindo.*

equally elaborate helmets, but in the Holy Roman Empire (centred on the German-speaking regions) no such contrived system of helmets developed. The German titled nobility used the grilled helmet but without any specific numbers of bars, while new nobility (down to the third generation) were supposed to use the closed helm. However, in the late 19th century, German and Scandinavian families of ancient lineage attempted to assert their superiority over the newly ennobled by setting their arms in the style of the 14th and 15th centuries, the helm being the great helm of that period.

The nobility of England knew only two styles of heraldic helmet. The barred helmet, in silver with gold bars, was given to the members of the peerage, or major nobility. Knights, baronets and gentlemen were given the plain steel closed helm, with the visor open for the first two degrees and closed for gentlemen.

CORONETS AND CROWNS

From the 14th century, crowns or jewelled circlets began to appear in the arms of many families, not only those of royal rank. At the same time, however, some documents of the age also show the arms

of rulers bearing crested helms without any distinguishing royal headgear. Crowns and coronets are common in heraldry, either above the shield or helm, or as charges.

Early heraldic coronets tended to be simplified versions of those worn by kings and princes. From a jewelled circlet rose a series of leaf-like embellishments, which in later centuries became formalized as fleurs de lis, strawberry leaves and other standard designs. The styles of coronets of rank among the aristocracy was set in the 16th and 17th centuries, although Europe's nobility had actually been wearing coronets for centuries.

The Renaissance brought with it an ever more formalized system of coronets, with tops constructed of specific numbers of leaves and pearls depending on the bearer's rank. In most cases these are heraldic conventions, and such designs were never actually worn. Southern European states took the heraldry of France as their model, while northern Europe looked to the Holy Roman Empire for styles and patterns.

The only nobility (as opposed to royalty) actually to wear their coronets were, and are, the British, where coronets are worn by peers on only one occasion – the coronation of the sovereign. At the moment of crowning the peers place their crowns on their heads. In recent times heraldic coronets have been designed for civic councils, not only in Europe but as far afield as Gabon in West Africa.

THE SUPPORTERS

Supporters, as their name suggests, are those heraldic accessories that support the shield of arms. They may be human figures, animals or mythical beasts, and very rarely they can also be inanimate objects. Supporters are by no means as common as the other components of a coat of arms, the shield, crest and helmet. They are mainly associated with the highest ranks of nobility and royalty. Various suggestions have been offered to explain the origins of heraldic supporters. One such

▲ *The seal of Gilles de Trazegnies, c1195, with its bear supporter.*

▼ *Angels supporting the arms of the Empire and Nuremberg, by Albrecht Dürer, 1521.*

▲ *An angel supporting a shield of arms on a medieval church roof – one of the possible origins of heraldic supporters.*

suggestion concerns the flights of angels that decorate many a medieval church roof. Often the angels hold symbols of saints or representations of the Passion, and some also support the shields of benefactors; perhaps the first supporters were echoing this device. Another explanation for the presence of supporters is as space fillers in the designs of medieval heraldic seals. In this context, supporters were a delightful conceit by which the seal engraver could avoid any large blank areas, which would not imprint well. An example of this is the seal of Gilles de Trazegnies, which shows his shield of arms suspended over the shoulders of a bear by its guige (the strap used to suspend the shield when not needed in battle). This seal has been dated to 1195, one of the earliest instances of a heraldic supporter. Almost half the seals of

▼ *The wildmen supporters of the Kingdom of Prussia, with traditional oak leaf nether garments and headgear.*

English barons found on a letter to the pope dating from 1300–1 have complex designs with Gothic-style archings and piercings. The spaces between these patterns and the shield are filled with dragons, lions or similar charges; often pairs of the creatures appear to be resting on the edge of the shield – very much like the supporters of a century or two later.

Supporters in the form of monsters – usually human figures of ferocious appearance, such as giants or wild men of the woods – could well have their origins in the fantastical displays put on during tournaments and pageants sponsored by noble participants. The knights would have their entrance announced by their servants, who would be dressed up for the occasion in the most fanciful of costumes.

HUMAN FIGURES

Since most members of the nobility of Europe like to trace their ancestry back to a warrior forebear, it is not surprising to find military figures supporting the shields of many titled families. Human supporters have been adapted to suit the period and the profession of the bearer, but possibly the most curious warrior supporters are two Augustinian friars, each bearing a sword, belonging to one of the princes of Monaco. They commemorate the legendary capture of Monaco in 1297 by

▼ *Francisco Grimaldi and his companion, both disguised as Augustinians, supporting the shield of the princes of Monaco.*

Francisco Grimaldi and his companions, who disguised themselves as Augustinians and thereby utterly surprised the garrison.

Soldiers often appear as supporters to commemorate a battle or campaign in which an ancestor proved himself. Such supporters are popular in British and Russian heraldry and Hungarian hussars support the shields of various Hungarian counts. Armoured knights were very popular in the 18th and early 19th centuries.

OTHER SUPPORTERS

In the Holy Roman Empire, some cities with rights of free trade and exemption from certain taxes bore their arms on the imperial *Doppeladler* (double-headed eagle). The families of high-ranking nobles – counts and princes of the Holy Roman Empire – also often bore their arms on the breast of this creature, surely one of the most impressive charges in the entire heraldic menagerie. Few English families were entitled to the use of the imperial eagle, associated as it was with a Catholic monarchy, but the Dukes of Marlborough and Earls Cowper (both princes of the Holy Roman Empire) and the Barons Arundell of Wardour made use of the right, with licence from the British monarch.

The grandest creature of all must be the *Quaternionenadler*, emblem of the Holy Roman Empire between the 15th century and 17th century. Here the double-headed eagle was fully displayed, with each pinion of its wings bearing a group of four shields representing the empire's lands.

▼ *The curious supporters of the counts de Grave – peacocks with human faces.*

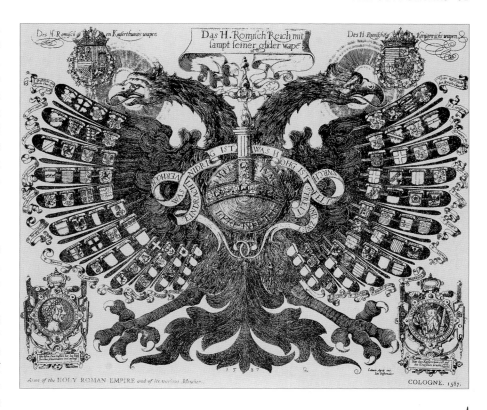

Curious marriages of monster and man also arise, surely none more exotic than the human-faced peacock supporters of the de Grave family in France.

Most supporters are borne in pairs, but this is by no means the rule. An early example of a single supporter is the goat-headed eagle of Count Gottfried of Ziegenhain (*Ziege* is the German word for goat) of the late 14th century. A branch of the Scottish family of Campbell has the unique distinction of placing its arms in front of a Scottish heraldic ship, the "lymphad". This was probably adapted from a similar vessel found in the arms of Lorne, which were also quartered by the Campbells.

Rarer than the single supporter are multiple supporters. Of these, the most curious example appears on the arms of the d'Albret family, former Constables of France. For this heraldic balancing act, the supporters are two lions, each wearing a helmet and supporting an eagle. A more modern example of multiple supporters was granted in 1981 to Air Chief Marshal Sir John Davis, Knight Grand Cross of the Order of the Bath. The supporters are two black eagles, but also, under the wing of one, a young eaglet appears, representing

▲ *The double-headed eagle of the Holy Roman Empire, 1587, the wings charged with groupings of shields.*

► *The statue of a heraldic salmon supporting the arms of Greystock, made for Thomas, Lord Dacre (1467–1526).*

Sir John's former position as chief officer overseeing training of aircrews.

MODERN TRENDS

In England and Wales, supporters are currently granted only to peers of the realm, Knights of the Garter, Grand Cross, of the Orders of the Bath, St Michael and St George, the British Empire and the Royal Victoria Order. In Scotland supporters are granted to the Knights of the Thistle and holders of old feudal titles.

In recent years the British House of Lords

▲ *An unusual case of a single supporter: the heraldic ship of the Campbells of Craignish.*

▼ *The supporters of the d'Albrets perform a heraldic balancing act.*

▼ *A mother eagle guards its fledgling – the allusive supporters (dexter) of the late Air Chief Marshal, Sir John Davis, GCB.*

has seen the exodus of most hereditary peers, who have been replaced by an increasing number of life peers. This wind of change has been reflected in the nature of the heraldic supporters granted to the "lifers", who often eschew traditional creatures such as lions, wyverns, dragons and griffins. In their place stand more personal figures such as family pets, for when life peers die so also do their supporters.

The crime writer, P. D. James, now Baroness James of Holland Park, has two tabby cats to support her lozenge of arms. Baroness Perry of Southwark, another fan of the feline species, also decided on two cats for her supporters – a tabby tom and a Persian female. The latter is depicted standing on a pile of books, as she is

▶ *A traditional choice of supporters – a lion and a stag – is depicted in the decadent Rococo style. The animals' general lack of interest means the shield isn't actually supported at all.*

▲ *A British bulldog and an American bald eagle as supporters celebrate the marriage of an Englishman – Lord Hanson – and his American wife.*

not as big as the tabby. Dogs, too, have their day in the modern world of heraldry. Lord Cobbold chose for his supporters two golden labradors based on his own pets. Since Lord Cobbold is a hereditary peer, unusually his dog supporters will descend in the male line so long as the family continues.

▲ *The arms of Baroness Perry, showing her domestic cat supporters.*

THE COMPARTMENT

Beneath the shield, placed as if to give supporters a foothold or resting place, is an object known as the compartment. Although instances of animal and human supporters lodged in parks or on mounds are known from the late medieval period, the compartment seems mainly to have been a product of the Renaissance, when heraldic artists expressed the artistic motivation of the age by showing the arms in

▼ *In the achievement of the Old Town of Belgrade, the supporters stand on a battlemented compartment.*

elaborate frameworks, with the shield and supporters placed on splendid pedestals decorated with classical motifs, masks, foliate symbols and strapwork. Later artistic periods lent their styles to shield supporters and compartment alike.

By the 19th century the compartment had largely been reduced to a piece of metalwork looking rather like a bracket for an old gas lamp, with the heraldic supporters performing a rather precarious balancing act. Even more common was the use of the paper scroll as a platform, upon which stood horses, griffins, or even elephants.

Royal burghs of Scotland are entitled to stand their heraldic supporters on a special compartment that is formed of turretted and embattled masonry, often with the motto set in a plaque in the compartment, something copied in arms of the Old Town of Belgrade.

In recent years, the Canadian Heraldic Authority has included in many of its grants of arms to civic and regional authorities, compartments that reflect the geography, flora and even fish of the area. The supporters of the City of White Rock, for example, stand on a white rock charged with two forts, while the arms of the

▲ *Kangaroos support the shield of the Australian Northern Territory on a compartment of sand.*

Canadian Heraldic Authority itself rest on a compartment strewn with two maple leaves. The Authority's most curious innovation is its amalgamation of compartment and single supporter by placing a shield on a cathedra, or bishop's chair.

The English heralds have been granting compartments for some years, one of the most unusual being the arms granted to the Northern Territory of Australia in 1978. The grant of arms quotes the compartment as having a "grassy sandy mound", the shield of arms takes the brown colour of the local earth and bears the following charges: "Aboriginal rock paintings including a woman with styled internal anatomy".

▼ *The arms of Canada's cathedral churches show an interesting combination of the single supporter and the compartment.*

MOTTOES AND INSCRIPTIONS

The coat of arms often includes a word or short sentence known as the motto. The position of the motto is somewhat nebulous compared to that of the shield of arms and crest. In England, where it appears below the shield, it is not even mentioned in a grant of arms and can be changed at will. Most mottoes are of relatively recent origin. In Scotland, however, the motto is considered a hereditary item much in the manner of the arms and crest, and is therefore mentioned in grants and matriculation of arms.

ANCIENT WAR CRIES

The motto probably has its origin in the *cri-de-guerre* or war cry of medieval warlords, used to rally their retinues and imbue in them a sense of loyal pride and bravura. In this league are the mottoes of the great Irish families of Butler and FitzGerald, who respectively rallied to their chiefs under the calls of *Butler a boo*, and *Crom a boo*. "A boo" was the Erse cry to victory, and Croom Castle a principal property of the FitzGeralds.

Scottish mottoes, which appear above the crest, are very much in the manner of the ancient war cry. Among the most famous are *Gang warily* of the earls of Perth,

▼ *The famous war cry of the Dukes of Leinster,* Crom a boo, *was later adopted as the motto on their arms.*

▲ *The simple* Through *motto of the Dukes of Hamilton is depicted above the crest in typical Scottish fashion.*

and *Through* of Hamilton, and the less familiar but curious *Beware in time* of Lumsden of Innergelly, and *Enough in my hand* of Cunningham of Cunninghamhead, which is borne above the crest of a hand bearing the upper part of an anchor. Other branches of the Cunningham family bear *Over fork over* and their arms are charged with their famous "shakefork". This is said to commemorate one of the family who, while fleeing enemies, disguised himself as a farmworker forking hay. Mesmerized by the closeness of his foes, he nearly gave himself away until a companion whispered in his ear the words that now provide the family motto. Like many similar picturesque tales, they were almost certainly invented to give an ordinary heraldic charge a noble origin.

Among the abundant references to the bloody history of the Scots crown in the heraldry of that nation's noble families, are the crest and motto of Kirkpatrick. The crest – a hand holding a bloody dagger – and the motto *I mak sikker* ("I make sure"), refer to the supposed outcome of a feud between Robert the Bruce and Red Comyn. Robert the Bruce managed to wound Comyn but the deed was finished by Bruce's follower, Kirkpatrick, who made the fatal thrust with his own dagger.

The motto of the Robertsons of Struan is *Virtutis gloria merces*, "Glory is the reward of valour." Like the crest – a hand grasping a crown – it refers to the capture in 1437 of the murderers of King James I by Robertson, the Chief of Clan Donnachaidh. An unconventional and unexplained feature of the arms is the figure of a naked man, chained and manacled, lying beneath the shield.

A curious happening is responsible for the motto *Prenez harleine tirez fort*, "Take aim and shoot strongly", borne to this day by the ancient family of Giffard of Chillington in Staffordshire, along with the two crests of a panther's head and an archer with a quiver of arrows and a drawn bow. They commemorate an event on the Giffard estate when Sir John Giffard was teaching his young son archery. A panther, a gift to Sir John, had escaped and was about to attack a woman and her baby. Sir John told his son to take aim with his bow and arrow. The lad did so, but with obvious trepidation, so Sir John whispered in his ear the words that became the family's motto. The boy did take aim, fired strongly, and according to legend, managed to kill the panther with a single shot.

▼ *The two crests of a bowman and a panther belong to the Giffards of Chillington.*

▲ *The arms of Sigismondo Malatesta, Lord of Rimini, make a heraldic statement of the love he bore his lady, Isotta degli Atti.*

▲ *The arms of the Manrique de Lara family of Spain bear their proud motto.*

PIETY AND AFFIRMATION

Many mottoes urge both onlooker and bearer to espouse Christian values or even, as in that of the great French family of Montmorency – *Dieu ayde au primer baron chrestien* – to ask God to assist the family. Others affirm the nobility of the line, among them being *Let Curzon hold what Curzon held* of the Curzons of Kedleston in England (whose estate has remained in the family from the Norman Conquest until the present day), and the splendid *Nos non venimos de reyes, que reyes vienen de nos* of the great Castilian family of Manrique de Lara, which asserts "we do not come from kings, kings come from us".

INSCRIPTIONS ON THE SHIELD

Letters and words used as charges on the shield are not uncommon but tend to be frowned upon by many in the heraldic world as inauthentic. Nevertheless, letters and words are often used for the proudest reason, the "SPQR" (*Senatus Populusque Romanus*) of the Roman Empire being the most famous case. During the Renaissance, the rulers of northern Italy often combined their family arms with their ciphers, but the great mercenary general Sigismondo Malatesta went one better. He quartered his arms with his own initials and with those of his lover, Isotta degli Atti.

A lettered shield, worthy of remark, is that in the former arms of the island of Saaremaa in Estonia. In the first half of the

16th century the island's ruler, Bishop Johannes Kievel, was an admirer of Duke Friedrich III of Saxony, protector of Martin Luther. Consequently, he gave to Saaremaa a shield bearing the letters "DWGBE", the initial letters of Duke Friedrich's personal motto *De wort Gottes blist ewig*, "The word of God endureth forever".

▲ *In a statement of sovereignty, Vespasius Gonzaga, Duke of Sabbioneta, acclaims the freedom of his little state from the parent duchy of Mantua.*

▲ *As a statement of loyalty, Bishop Johannes IV Kievel remembers the motto of Duke Friedrich III of Saxony on the shield of the island of Saaremaa.*

THE LANGUAGE OF HERALDRY

Many people are baffled by the language used by heraldists in the English-speaking world. In many countries it relies heavily on Norman French, the language of William the Conqueror, which was spoken by the nobility in much of Europe during the period when heraldry was evolving. To take one example, "Vert three estoiles Or" would be the correct way to describe a green shield upon which were three gold stars with wavy rays, yet none of the descriptive words are English. In other nations, such as Germany, heraldic language is much nearer to modern-day usage.

The language of heraldry is known in the English-speaking world as "blazonry", from the old German word *blasen,* meaning to blow a horn. At a tournament, it was the duty of the medieval herald to call out the names, titles, genealogy and arms of the participating knights, accompanied by a flourish of trumpets, and the word thus also came to mean a public proclamation.

◀ *The unusual crest of the Davenport family of Capesthorne, England, showing an anonymous felon on his way to execution.*

COLOURS, METALS AND FUR

Heraldic language – no less vivid than the contrasting colours and bright metals of heraldry itself – paints a word picture of the luxurious accoutrements of medieval nobles. The terms suggest exotic and costly goods imported from the far corners of the known world, such as sable – the sleek, black fur of the marten, brought by merchants from far-off Muscovy – or gules, the rose-red dye produced in Persia and Turkey. The general term used to define all colours and textures on a shield of arms is equally picturesque and evocative: colours, metals and furs are together known as "tinctures", a word that at one time meant a dye or tint.

COLOURS AND METALS

To begin the "blazoning", or description in heraldic terms, of any shield of arms, it is necessary to deal with colour, since the very first word used in the description refers to the colour of the background or "field"

▲ *Two good examples of the reason behind the rule against colour on colour. From a distance identification would be very difficult.*

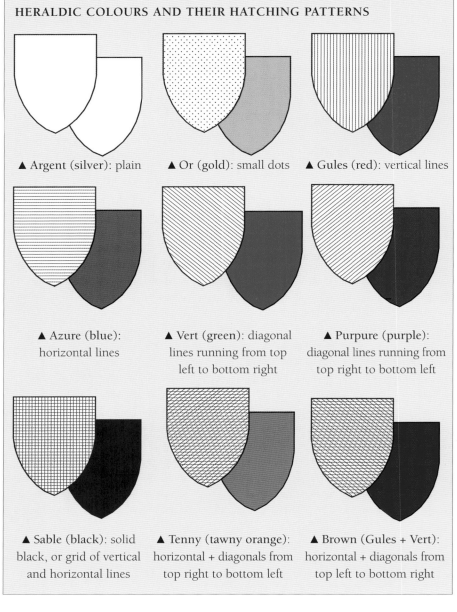

HERALDIC COLOURS AND THEIR HATCHING PATTERNS

▲ **Argent (silver): plain**

▲ **Or (gold): small dots**

▲ **Gules (red): vertical lines**

▲ **Azure (blue): horizontal lines**

▲ **Vert (green): diagonal lines running from top left to bottom right**

▲ **Purpure (purple): diagonal lines running from top right to bottom left**

▲ **Sable (black): solid black, or grid of vertical and horizontal lines**

▲ **Tenny (tawny orange): horizontal + diagonals from top right to bottom left**

▲ **Brown (Gules + Vert): horizontal + diagonals from top left to bottom right**

of the shield. There are five main colours in heraldry (although this differs slightly from nation to nation): red, blue, black, green and purple. Some mixed colours, known as stains, are also sometimes used. The two metals – gold and silver – are usually depicted as yellow and white. In British heraldry Norman French names are used for colours and metals, though gold and silver are also sometimes used in blazonry instead of "Or" and "Argent".

The colour green has intrigued heraldic writers for centuries. Some suggest that it was actually unknown in early heraldry, yet one of the earliest compilations of arms, illustrating the *Historia Anglorum* (written between 1250–59 by an English cleric, Matthew Paris) clearly shows the shield of one of chivalry's greatest names, William Marshal, with a field of gold and green.

THE RULE OF TINCTURES

An important heraldic principle governs the use of colours and metals: "Never place a colour on a colour or a metal on a metal". It is a very sensible rule, remembering that the original purpose of heraldry was quick and ready identification on the battlefield. Life could depend on it. A blue charge on a black field, for example, or gold on silver, would be difficult to distinguish in the melée of medieval warfare. However, as long as the charge lies partly on an opposite – such as a red lion on a field of gold and blue – this does not constitute a breaking of the rule.

The rule is not strictly observed in some countries, and Archbishop Bruno Heim in his book *Or and Argent* (1994) gives many examples of gold charges on a white field, the most famous being the arms of Jerusalem. Some heraldic writers have suggested, however, that the gold crosses on this shield were originally red, but that medieval painting methods and materials caused the red to oxidize, causing later heraldists to mistake the original colour.

HERALDIC FURS

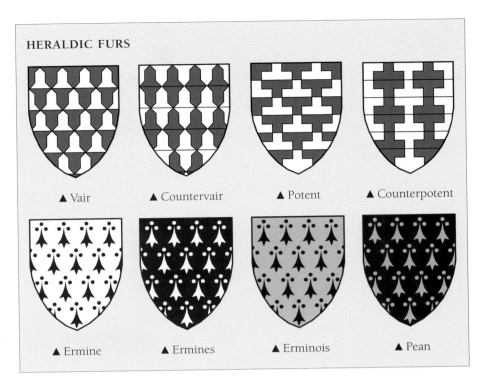

▲ Vair ▲ Countervair ▲ Potent ▲ Counterpotent

▲ Ermine ▲ Ermines ▲ Erminois ▲ Pean

▲ *The arms of Jerusalem, an exception to the rule against metal on metal, possibly allowed because of the holiness of the city.*

FURS

In addition to the colours and metals, heraldry makes use of "furs" – patterns that suggest the costly furs worn by the medieval nobility. The two main furs are "ermine" and "vair", and each has several derivatives. Fur, just like a coloured field, can have any variety of charges placed upon it, and can take the place of either metal or colour.

Ermine is the highly prized winter fur of the common stoat. The animal's coat changes colour from chestnut brown to white except for the tip of its tail, which remains black. In heraldry, ermine is shown as a white field strewn with little black tail-tips, usually accompanied by

three black dots, which represent the fastenings by which the pelts were sewn into a robe. Ermine by itself constitutes the arms of the dukes of Brittany and makes a simple but splendid appearance in *The Book of Tourneys* of King René of Anjou.

Vair is indicated by a white and blue pattern said to represent the pelts of a species of squirrel, the blue-grey fur from its back arranged alternately with the paler fur from its underbelly. Vair was the arms of the Beauchamp family of Somerset, England and is often included in the quarterings of Henry VIII's wife, Jane Seymour.

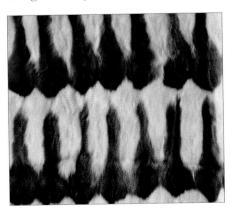

▲ *A real piece of vair, the fur made from the backs and fronts of squirrel pelts sewn into a warm and handsome covering, from which the heraldic fur is derived.*

HATCHING AND TRICKING

It is, of course, not always possible to use colour in depictions of arms, and various methods of identifying heraldic colours in black and white have been used. The two most common are known as "hatching" and "tricking". Silvestro de Petra Sancta, a 17th-century Jesuit writer, devised the method of showing colours represented by lines and dots, which was later named hatching, and which has been universally adopted.

A simple description of a shield of arms can also be made by tricking: this involves annotating a sketch of the arms with abbreviations for each colour, as in the example shown below. In this system azure becomes "az", gules "gu" and so on.

▲ *An example of the tricking of a crest, where the colours are denoted by letters representing the heraldic tinctures.*

THE DIVISION OF THE FIELD

The entire surface of the heraldic shield is known as the field, and its tincture is always described first in blazonry. It is said that the simplest arms are the best, and indeed there have been cases where an ancient family has borne for its arms a shield of just a single plain colour. The most famous example is probably the noble French family of d'Albret, which bore a shield simply Gules, while the English knight, Sir Thomas Holland (1320–60) abandoned his ancient family arms in favour of a plain shield Sable.

Of course, to allow for the numerous variations needed to ensure that every shield is unique, a more elaborate scheme is usually required. Any number of motifs, known as charges, may be placed on the field, from basic geometric shapes to representations of any object, animate or inanimate. Whether or not charges appear, the field may be divided into sections of different colours.

DESCRIBING THE DIVISIONS

When the shield is divided, or "parted", into various simple divisions or blocks, this is signalled by the words "party per", (divided by) or more simply "per", followed by the particular nature of the division, such as "party per chevron" (divided by a chevron) or "party per pale" (divided in half vertically). The descriptions of the

▲ *In the later version of the d'Albret family arms, the 2nd and 3rd quarters are the original arms – here hatched to represent gules – and the 1st and 4th quarters were augmented by the King of France.*

divisions utilize the names given to the corresponding "ordinaries" – the fundamental geometric charges (see opposite). Where the shield is parted in an even number of small divisions the number of divisions is then specified, such as "bendy of six"; "paly of eight"; "barry of ten". Any parted field can bear another charge or charges of either a metal or a colour, without breaking the metal-on-metal, colour-on-colour rule.

In spite of their simplicity, it is quite possible for one of these basic divisions of the shield to comprise a family arms. For at least 650 years, the ancient English family of Waldegrave has used a shield that is simply Per pale Argent and Gules (a shield divided in half, one half silver, one half red). The Scottish dukes of Argyll, Chiefs of the Clan Campbell, bear Gyronny of eight Or and Sable; the Campbells of London bear Gyronny of eight ermine and Gules, and the Swedish family of Natt och Dag ("night and day") derived its name from its simple shield Per fess Or and Azure (divided in two horizontally, one half blue for night and one half gold for day).

DIAPERING

Where a shield has a large expanse of field, the artist often adds textural interest with a faint overall pattern. This technique is called "diapering", and can lead to the most beautiful of heraldic art forms as long as the pattern is not mistaken for part of the heraldic design.

▼ *The field of the Fisher family of Lancashire is diapered with little fishes.*

SHIELD DIVISIONS

The simplest way of creating arms that are distinct from any other, is to divide the surface of the shield into two parts by a line, one part a metal – gold or silver – the other a colour. Further variations can be made by subdividing the shield with more lines, and varying the edges of the lines in many ways. The option of adding furs to the variations makes the possibilities for new but simple geometric designs almost endless.

▲ (Party) per pale

▲ (Party) per fess

▲ (Party) per bend

▲ (Party) per bend sinister

▲ (Party) per chevron

▲ (Party) per saltire

▲ Tierced per pale

▲ Tierced per fess

▲ Quarterly

▲ Gyronny

▲ Barry (six)

▲ Bendy (six)

▲ Bendy sinister

▲ Paly

▲ Chevronny

▲ Chequy

▲ Lozengy

▲ Barry bendy

▲ Paly bendy

▲ Gyronny of twelve

▲ Pily

▲ Pily bendy

▲ Pily bendy sinister

THE HONOURABLE ORDINARIES

The most simple charges, or devices, found on the heraldic shield are geometric patterns called the ordinaries. These charges have long been considered to hold a special place in heraldry, hence the appellation "honourable". The ordinary normally occupies about one-third of the area of the shield, and can be borne alone or in conjunction with other charges. It can also itself bear further charges. In blazonry, the ordinary is always mentioned directly after the field.

Various theories about the origins of the ordinaries have been put forward, including the fanciful suggestion that the chevron, for example, is a charge suitable for the head of a family who gives shelter to other family members. An interesting but unexplained visual clue lies in a Roman mosaic representing the amphitheatre of Lyons in France (and now in the city's museum). The mosaic shows a wooden palisade around the arena that contains many of the ordinaries and subordinaries found in heraldry. Whether there is a link between a Roman geometrical conceit and heraldry, or if it is just a curious coincidence is still debated.

VARIATIONS ON THE ORDINARIES

Some of the ordinaries, such as the bands, can also be borne in smaller forms in pairs or more. These diminutive ordinaries have names that reflect their nature, so that chevrons give rise to chevronels, pales to pallets and two or more bends are described as bendlets. Any ordinary can be "voided" by having its centre removed to reveal the field or another tincture; it can also be "fimbriated", that is, edged with a narrow band of another tincture.

THE CROSS

The heraldic cross is formed by a combination of the "fess" (horizontal band) and the "pale" (vertical band). In its simple form it is set centrally on the shield, with each limb extending to one edge. The cross has bred more variants than any other

THE ORDINARIES
Although various writers quibble about the exact number of ordinaries, the following selection, with their diminutives behind them, is generally considered to be a complete list:

▲ The chief

▲ The pale and pallets

▲ Fess ▲ 2 bars ▲ A barrulet

▲ Bend ▲ 3 bendlets ▲ A riband

▲ Bend sinister ▲ 2 bendlets sinister

▲ Chevron ▲ 3 chevronels

▲ Saltire ▲ A fillet saltire

▲ Pall ▲ A fillet pall

▲ Cross ▲ A fillet cross

▲ Pile ▲ 3 piles in point

charge: some writers say there are over 30 variants, others over 50, while one 19th-century writer listed 450. Apart from the simple cross the most commonly met with are the "cross" patty (or "formy") where the four limbs are wide at their heads but narrow towards the central join, and the Maltese or eight-pointed cross, which is similar to the former except that the heads of the limbs are notched at their centres. If the bottom limb of the cross narrows to a point it is said to be "fitched". Crosses patty and "crosslet" can often be found with this variant, and are then described as a "cross patty fitchy" or a "cross crosslet fitchy".

▶ *A Flemish armorial, c1560, showing ordinaries and divisions of the field.*

VARIATIONS ON THE CROSS

▲ Cross potent: T-shaped limbs, resembling crutches.

▲ Cross patonce: Concave, tapered limbs, with each head divided into three.

▲ Cross fleury or flory: the accentuated points end in the form of a fleur de lis.

▲ Cross crosslet: The heads of each limb are themselves crossed.

▲ Cross bottony: Straight limbs, each headed with three roundels or buttons.

▲ Formy (Patty)

▲ Maltese

▲ Moline

▲ Pommée

▲ Fleuretty

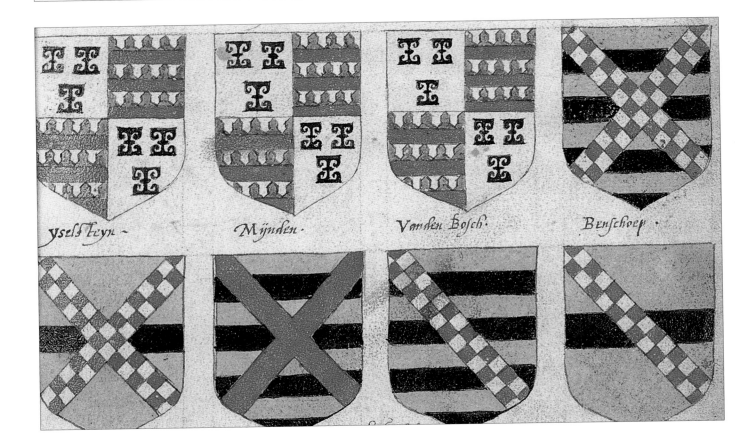

THE SUB-ORDINARIES

The lesser geometric charges are known as the "sub-ordinaries"; they can be borne singly or in groups according to their nature. The sub-ordinaries are deemed the less common of the geometric patterns found on shields of arms, but like many of the honourable ordinaries, most of them owe their origins to the construction of the medieval shield.

The most non-controversial sub-ordinaries are the "canton" (and its larger cousin, the quarter), the "bordure", the "inescutcheon", the "orle" and the "tressure". The last four are probably reminders of metal reinforcements that were part of the structure of the medieval shield. Other writers have also included further charges in the list of the sub-ordinaries, including the "lozenge" and its derivatives, the "rustre", "mascle", and "fusil", the "gyron", the "pairle", the "billet" and "flanches".

The bordure, or border, is simply that: a border around the edge of the shield. In Scottish heraldry the bordure is often used as a means of identifying junior branches of the family, the bordure bearing charges taken from the arms of the mother (see Difference Marks and Cadency). A similar practice is found in Spanish and Portuguese heraldry, where the bordure may even include small shields of arms of near relatives.

The inescutcheon is a small shield borne as a charge. It may be plain or may bear other charges and may be in any number, not just single. The arms of Burrell, Baron Gwydir, make use of this and another sub-ordinary, blazoned Vert on each of three escutcheons Argent a bordure engrailed Or, while the family of Hay, Earl of Erroll, High Constable of Scotland, are blazoned Argent three escutcheons Gules.

The orle appears as an inner border set between the middle and edge of the shield. French heraldists also call it a faux, or false, escutcheon, or inescutcheon voided.

The tressure is really little more than a narrow orle and often appears in pairs in Scottish heraldry where, garnished with fleurs de lis, it is usually associated with the royal arms of Scotland and other families allied to the Scottish monarchy through marriage.

The canton is a square or rectangle in the dexter chief corner of the shield, smaller than the less-common quarter. The canton often bears other charges and in the heraldry of some nations can be used to denote certain relationships.

Flanches are always borne in pairs, and are formed by arcs on each side of the shield extending from the upper corner to a point slightly to the side of the base.

The lozenge is a diamond-shaped charge that has several variants, the most common being the mascle – a lozenge with its centre removed to show the field. A rustre is a lozenge pierced with a circular opening, and a fusil is an elongated lozenge. A field patterned overall with lozenges is "lozengy"; with squares it is "chequy".

A billet is a small elongated rectangular

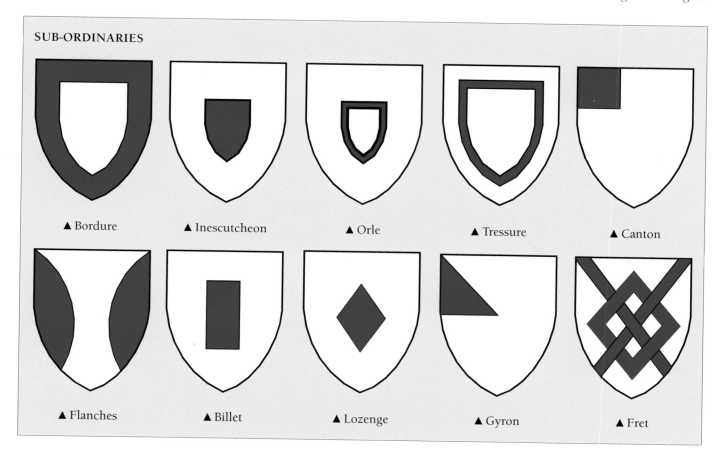

SUB-ORDINARIES

▲ Bordure   ▲ Inescutcheon   ▲ Orle   ▲ Tressure   ▲ Canton

▲ Flanches   ▲ Billet   ▲ Lozenge   ▲ Gyron   ▲ Fret

figure. Numerous billets are often strewn across the field, described as "billety".

The gyron is a triangular charge that seldom appears singly. Usually the shield is divided into a number of gyrons, arranged like the sails of a windmill, and the field is described as "gyronny of [the number of pieces]". The most famous example of a gyronny coat is that of the Scottish family of Campbell, who bear Gyronny of eight Or and Sable. Branches of the family often charge the gyrons with other charges or vary their edges and colours.

The "fret" is formed of interlaced bendlets and bendlets sinister. It can be encountered in the singular but is more often repeated to cover the whole field in an interlacing pattern, which resembles a garden trellis; this is then described as "fretty".

OVERALL PATTERNS

Generally, if charges are repeated on a shield, their number tends to be less than ten, and is specified in the blazon. Furthermore, they are usually placed within the perimeter of the shield so that they appear in their entirety. Sometimes, however, small charges – which may be of any kind – are strewn in a plentiful degree all over the shield. This effect is described as "semy".

There are special terms for the strewing of certain charges. For example, a shield strewn with billets is billety and one strewn with fleur de lis is semy de lis. Any object, no matter how humble or curious, can be strewn across the shield – such as semy of coffee beans in the arms of the district of Haut Ogooué in Gabon.

ROUNDELS

Plain round charges called "roundels" are depicted in heraldic colours and metals. Whereas in most heraldics the roundel is described simply in its true colour, English blazonry has a distinct name for each roundel. The "bezant", or gold roundel, is said to be named after the gold coin of Byzantium, while the "torteau", or red roundel, resembles a tartlet. A blue roundel is a "hurt", which may refer either to a bruise or to a hurtleberry (blueberry). Droplets are a variation of the roundel, and look something like tadpoles. They are known as "gouttés". Once again, in English heraldry Norman French is utilized: red droplets are goutté de sang – drops of blood – gold droplets are goutté d'or. A roundel bearing blue and white wavy bars is often used to denote water: this is termed the "fountain". It is seen in the arms of the Sykes family, since a "syke" is a spring or fountain.

The English family of Stourton makes use of fountains and a bend to tell the story of their ancient estate. Six springs rise at Stourhead, forming the source of the River Stour: three were originally inside the estate boundary, the other three outside. The Stourton arms, Sable a bend Or between six fountains, neatly describes the geography and history of the estate.

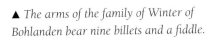

▲ The arms of the family of Winter of Bohlanden bear nine billets and a fiddle.

▲ In a novel use of semy, the chief in the shield of the Gabonaise region of Haut Ogooué is semy of coffee beans.

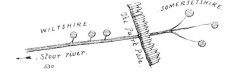

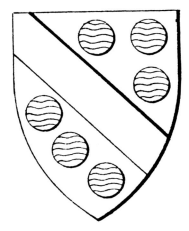

▲ The six fountains and bend in the arms of the Stourton family reflect the positions of six springs on the family property. A sketch-map above explains the pattern.

LINES OF PARTITION

Heraldry is nothing if not inventive and over the centuries its regulators have come up with every possible method to ensure that each shield of arms can be unique. This is especially true of the many ways that a shield can be divided. To increase the number of possible variations, the edges of the divisions and the ordinaries, which are known as "lines of partition", can be drawn in many different styles.

Partition lines make the fullest use of the edges of the ordinaries and they are considered sufficiently distinctive for unrelated families to have a coat of arms that is identical in colour and ordinary, but with different edges. For example, a green cross with straight edges on a white shield may belong to a family unrelated to one whose white shield bears a green cross with wavy edges. In fact, lines are included in the blazon only if they are not straight.

Apart from the styles shown here, in recent years new lines of partition have been evolved by the heraldic artists of Scandinavia, South Africa and Canada.

COUNTERCHANGING

One of the most enjoyable stratagems in blazon is a partitioned shield that is counterchanged. Counterchanging is the

▲ *Counterchanging is shown in practice on the shield of a community in Greenland. The shield is divided per fess.*

COMMON LINES OF PARTITION

The following shields show a selection of the many ways in which the heraldic division can be varied.

▲ **Engrailed:** scalloped, points facing outwards.

▲ **Invected:** as engrailed, points facing inwards.

▲ **Dancetty:** large saw-like points.

▲ **Indented:** small saw-like points.

▲ **Wavy:** like a wave.

▲ **Embattled/crenelly:** like battlements.

▲ **Nebuly:** cloudlike.

▲ **Raguly:** loglike.

▲ **Dovetailed**

▲ **Rayonné:** like flames.

▲ **Urdy:** serrated.

dividing of the shield in such a manner that it is part of a metal and part of a colour, and then by arranging the charges in such a manner that they be reciprocally of the same colour and metal. This sounds a complicated business, but counterchanging can in fact be one of the simplest and most effective ways of varying one very simple shield of arms from another.

The arms of the Anglo-Norman family of d'Abitot provide an example of how counterchanging can produce a striking design. The d'Abitot arms are Per pale Or and Gules three roundels counterchanged. They should be compared with the non-counterchanged alternatives, which are the arms of the Courtenay family (Or three torteaux) and its opposite, the arms of Dynham (Gules three bezants).

These three personal shields show how a certain configuration of charges can be changed through tincture. The families to which each shield belongs most probably bore no relation to each other, although changes of tincture were also sometimes employed for different members of the same family.

In the case of the Courtenay arms we can see how exact blazonry can be, the roundels each given its particular name, ie red roundels torteaux, and in the Dynham arms, gold roundels or bezants. Finally the d'Abitot arms combine these two designs but come up with something entirely different, by counterchanging both the field and the intersecting third roundel, resulting in a very distinctive shield.

EUROPEAN VARIANTS OF LINES OF PARTITION

Certain charges, divisions of the shield, partition lines and so on, are peculiar to a particular area or nation. In 1886, in his work entitled *Heraldry English and Foreign*, Robert Jenkins gave the following examples of variants and the names of some ordinaries that would seldom, if ever, be met with in English heraldry.

FAMILY ARMS

▲ Van Zirn   ▲ D'Arpo   ▲ Fromberg   ▲ Von Tale

▲ Kauffungen   ▲ Gleisenthal   ▲ Lindeck   ▲ Kunige

FRENCH VARIANTS OF ORDINARIES

▲ Chevron Failli   ▲ Chevron Ployé   ▲ Chevron Enlassé   ▲ Bande Anchée

▲ *The shield of the Courtenay family: Or three torteaux.*

▲ *The Dynham shield – a reversed version of the Courtenay shield: Gules three bezants.*

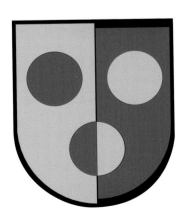

▲ *Finally the shield of the d'Abitots: Per pale Or and Gules three roundels counterchanged.*

BLAZONRY

The term blazonry refers to the special and distinct language that is used in the description of heraldry. Many a casual visitor to the world of heraldry can be baffled and put off by the nature of blazonry, but in fact it is a very user-friendly language, so exact in its phraseology that, once learnt, it enables one heraldist to impart to another an accurate and full description of any coat of arms through a concise verbal picture. Blazonry is a precise language, which it needs to be, for the nature of heraldry itself depends on the uniqueness of each coat of arms.

DESCRIBING A SHIELD

Any charge can be married to any other in any number of ways to make up a shield of arms. Often, the more ancient the arms, the simpler the design. It is in fact possible to have a shield of arms bearing no charges at all. The d'Albret arms were originally simply Gules (a plain red shield) though in 1389 they were "augmented" with the arms of France, becoming Quarterly one and four Azure three fleurs de lis Or two and three Gules (the shield was divided into four, quarters one and four were blue with three gold fleur de lis in each, quarters two and three remained the original red colour).

We have seen some of the fundamental charges employed in heraldry. Let us now see how they are "blazoned". The blazon needs to include all the details of tincture and number that an artist would need in order to reproduce the shield accurately. It always follows a set pattern:

1 The field, including any divisions
2 The ordinary
3 The principal charges on the field, followed by any lesser charges
4 Any charges on the ordinary
5 Any sub-ordinaries
6 Any charges on the sub-ordinaries
A further refinement of the language of blazonry is the means of describing the exact position on the shield any charge might take. The names of these parts and points of the shield are explained in the box.

THE PARTS AND POINTS OF THE SHIELD

For the purposes of accurate description, the heraldic shield is divided into different areas.

The dexter (right-hand) and sinister (left-hand) sides of the shield are always described from the point of view of the bearer of the shield, a throwback to the days when shields were actually carried. So from the reader's viewpoint, right is left and left is right. Most heraldic charges, particularly animate ones, are drawn so they are facing dexter, as it is considered the more "worthy" side. So from the point of the viewer, rather than a bearer, any lions, for example, on the shield, would usually face the left-hand side of the shield.

A B C: chief (top part of the shield), sub-divided into:
    A: dexter chief point
    B: middle chief point
    C: sinister chief point
D: honour point
E: fess or heart point
F: nombril or navel point
G H I: base, sub-divided into:
    G: dexter base point
    H: middle base point
    I: sinister base point

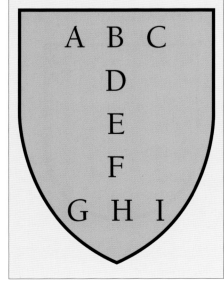

Here are three examples of how blazonry describes a shield. The first example is the arms of the family of Winneberg: Gules a bend Argent indented between six crosses couped Or.

1 The field is described first: Gules – a plain red background.

2 The next most important feature is the ordinary, in this case a bend Argent, noting any partition line, here indented.

3 Any lesser charges follow: between six crosses couped Or.

The arms of the town of Gerville, Seine-Maritime, France, is described as: Argent on a bend Azure between two Phrygian caps Gules three mullets of six points Or.

The more complex arms of the Johnson family, Suffolk, are described as: Sable on a fess between two double manacles Argent three pheons Gules on a chief Or a demi lion between two lozenges Azure.

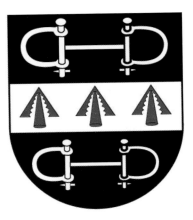

4 The charges, and their colour, on the ordinary are then described: three pheons [arrowheads] Gules.

1 The field is silver, the ordinary: on a bend Azure. ("On" anticipates point 3 below. As the lines of partition are straight they are not mentioned.)

1 The field: Sable.

2 The lesser charges on the field: between two Phrygian caps Gules.

2 The ordinary: on a fess.

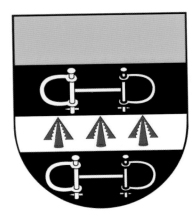

5 If a chief is borne in addition to another ordinary, as here, it is mentioned next: on a chief Or.

3 If any charges are borne on the ordinary, these are mentioned next: three mullets [stars] of six points Or.

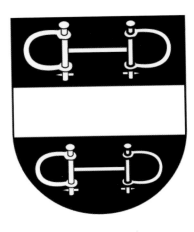

3 The lesser charges on the field: between two double manacles Argent. (As both fess and manacles are silver, the colour is mentioned only once.)

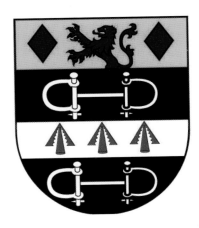

6 Any charges that appear on the chief now follow: a demi lion (the head and top half of a lion) between two lozenges Azure.

HERALDIC BEASTS

Although the earliest heraldry consisted mainly of simple geometric patterns – for easy identification at a distance – beasts, birds and monsters had begun to figure as emblems on shields and flags long before the birth of heraldry itself. We know that in ancient Greece the Athenians took an owl as their city's symbol. In ancient Egypt many of the gods were depicted partly or wholly in the forms of animals that lived alongside human beings, such as the jackal, cobra and hawk. The Bible records the instruction, "Every man of the children of Israel shall pitch by his own standard, with the ensign of their father's house" (Numbers 2:2), and of the 12 tribes of Israel no less than half took an animal as their symbol.

THE LION

Lions were in evidence at the very birth of heraldry – perhaps they were even the very first charge. When knighted in 1127 by his father-in-law, King Henry I of England, Geoffrey, Count of Anjou was given a shield bearing fanciful golden lions. The lion, believed to be the king of beasts, was

▼ *The lion, king of beasts: a page from a Dutch ordinary of 1570 shows family arms charged with the lion rampant.*

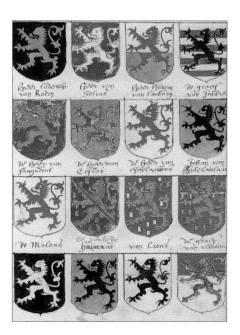

naturally a favourite symbol among the fighting men of medieval Europe, and was one of the more exotic beasts of the medieval heraldic menageries.

All postures or inclinations of an armorial charge are termed "attitudes", and this is especially relevant to creatures. Not surprisingly the lion is afforded the greatest number of attitudes – some writers have given it as many as 60 different positions. Besides its attitude, a lion or any other creature may also be distinguished by attributes. For example, a lion "passant" (attitude) may also be "langued" (tongued) in a tincture other than the normal red, and "armed" with teeth and claws.

Heraldry is an exact science. It needs to be if the individuality of a shield of arms is to be preserved, therefore attributes and attitudes are important. It could be that one family's blue shield bears a gold lion "rampant", another's a gold lion "rampant guardant" (looking at the viewer), while a third has a gold lion "rampant reguardant" (looking backwards): there is enough difference in the position of the head to give three distinct arms. Adding a forked tail ("queue fourchée") to the lions provides three more distinct arms.

OTHER BEASTS

Obviously many an early bearer of a lion chose the creature to reflect his own ferocity and bravery. The same may be said of those who chose bears, wolves and other carnivorous animals. Strength could be suggested by other creatures. The noble Moravian family of Pernstein bore on a white shield a black auroch's head "couped affronty" (with no neck visible, facing the viewer). According to a family legend the founding father of the Pernsteins was a charcoal burner of extraordinary strength called Vénava. He managed to catch a wild auroch and led it to the court of the king at Brno, where he cut off the poor beast's head with a single blow of his axe. The king was so impressed that he gave Vénava great estates and the right to commemorate his feat on his shield of arms.

▲ *This 1823 Bavarian grant of arms, to Baron Peter Kreusser, includes a variety of beasts from the heraldic menagerie.*

LIONS OR LEOPARDS

In 1235 the German emperor Frederick II presented Henry III of England with three leopards as a living shield of arms. Was this a reflection of the English arms at that time? If so, are the creatures in the English arms meant to be leopards? Confusion arises from the interpretation of heraldic terms describing the attitude of the lion. In English heraldry, the creature most often shown rearing up on one hind foot and boxing with its front paws is a lion "rampant", whereas if it is walking sedately across the shield it is a lion passant. In the arms of England the three lions are "passant guardant", walking and looking at the viewer. In French heraldry, the lion is always assumed to be rampant, while the creature that appears passant guardant is always a leopard. Furthermore, in French heraldry a rearing lion, looking at the viewer (in English "rampant guardant"), is called a *lion léopardé*, and a lion passant is a *léopard lionné*!

MOST COMMON ATTITUDES OF THE LION

▲ *Statant*

▲ *Combatant*

▲ *Rampant*

▲ *Rampant guardant*

▲ *Couchant*

▲ *Passant*

▲ *Salient*

▲ *Rampant double-queued*

▲ *Rampant reguardant*

▲ *Rampant queue fourchée*

▲ *Sejant*

▲ *Cowed*

▲ *A taste of the local flora and fauna from the Baltic States: left: Polvamaa, Estonia; middle: Balozi, Latvia; right: Auce, Latvia.*

Like many heraldic stories, it is impossible to know whether the auroch appeared on the Pernstein shield before or after the legend arose, but it is carved on the family's former castle at Pardubice.

While many men of warlike disposition would not have minded being represented by a bull, there must be few that would have chosen to bear its castrated equivalent, the ox. However, if Nicholas Upton, the 15th-century English heraldic writer, is to be believed, he was instrumental in the granting of a shield charged with three oxheads to a gentleman who had had the misfortune to have been maimed in the testicles by the thrust of a spear.

Another creature that Upton might have thought equally suitable for this client

▼ *A marvellous depiction carved in stone of the porcupine badge of King Louis XII of France (1498–1515), Chateau de Blois.*

would have been the beaver, whose scent glands, located near its rear, were sought after for various medicinal cures. Upton, along with other medieval writers, believed that these glands were in fact the beaver's testicles and that, when it realized that men were after them, it sensibly chose to sacrifice them by castrating itself with its teeth. Beavers, once common in much of Northern Europe, are now found only in the forests of Scandinavia and the Baltic States, and they appear in the arms of the Estonian district of Polvamaa.

Heraldry gives symbolic protection to all creatures, great and small, and whereas warriors might choose martial beasts such as lions, bears and wolves, country communities

▲ *The elephant in the arms of the Counts of Helfenstein, an unusual animal charge, was chosen as a delightful pun on the family's name.*

often prefer to commemorate gentler creatures. In Latvia, the rivers and forests yield up their wildlife to local heraldry. The arms of Auce – a black crayfish on a red field – enjoyably break the colour-on-colour rule. In the arms of Balozi a frog sits below a chief charged with water-lily leaves, while squirrels in the arms of Baldone and hedgehogs in those of Vilaka recall the creatures found in many gardens.

◄ *The arms of the Pernstein family of Moravia bear the popular bull's head as both a charge and a crest.*

▲ *Vénava kills his auroch in a relief carving at the family seat, the Castle of Pardubice.*

▲ *A camel appears in the arms of the city of Petropavlovsk, in the old Russian empire, where East met West.*

EXOTIC BEASTS

Of the more unusual animals, elephants were relatively well known to medieval heraldists (Henry III of England was given one for his menagerie by Louis IX of France in 1254). The elephant was used as a symbol of strength and dependability, and as such it was chosen for the arms of the city of Coventry in England. A particularly enjoyable example appears in the Zurich armorial roll (1335–45) for the von Helfenstein family of Swabia, chosen for its punning value with the family name.

Other exotic beasts in the heraldic menagerie include that of the eastern territories and cities of the old Russian Empire (such as Petropavlovsk) who favoured the camel in their civic heraldry, and when Sir Titus Salt, Baronet, of Saltaire, Yorkshire was granted arms, he chose as a crest the alpaca, from whose fine wool he had made his fortune.

ANIMAL PARTS

It is not only whole creatures that are used in heraldry; various parts of their anatomy make their way on to shields. Wolves' teeth famously appear on the Kinsky arms of Bohemia, while others include the bones of fish, and various types of amputations. The bits of animals that are all quite commonly used in heraldry include heads that are either "erased" (torn off at the neck) or "couped" (clean cut), various horns and antlers, and even the paws ("gambs") of bears and lions, which can also be either erased or couped.

DOMESTIC ANIMALS

Cats, dogs and horses are all corralled into heraldry, as are the unfortunate victims of the hunt: boar, deer, hares and rabbits. The stag hunt was for centuries the exclusive sport of the nobility, so it is no wonder that, after lions, deer probably appear most commonly upon shields and are therefore afforded the next largest group of personal attitudes. The English Cottington family enjoy two hinds in their arms "counter-tripping", which have the rather comical appearance of a Push-me-Pull-you.

Greyhounds are popular in Italian heraldry, while in British heraldry the talbot, a large and powerful ancient hunting hound, is often found. However, man's best friend comes no truer than the dog on the crest of a Mr Phillips of Cavendish Square, London, who early in the 19th century was swimming in the sea off Portsmouth when he got into a strong current and was in danger of being drowned. A perceptive Newfoundland hound saw his predicament, leapt into the water and dragged him to safety. When Mr Phillips found that his canine saviour was a stray, he took the brave dog home and gave him every kind attention that he deserved. Furthermore, the Phillips family recorded this happy outcome in a new heraldic crest and motto, the full blazon being: Upon a mount Vert in front of a Newfoundland dog sejant, reguardant proper an escutcheon thereon, in base waves of the sea, and floating therein a naked man, the sinister arm erected all proper. The motto is *Auspice Deo extuli mari*, "God being my leader, I brought him out of the sea".

▼ *In the arms of the English family of Sibell a tigress looks at herself in a mirror (3rd quarter). While she was beguiled by her own image her cubs were left unprotected.*

▼ *Stylized wolves' teeth appear on the shield of the Czech Count Kinsky, seen here on a beautifully crafted embellishment on a wrought-iron gate.*

▼ *Mr Phillips' faithful friend: the dog who saved his life and became his crest.*

HUMAN FIGURES

Human beings – and parts of them – appear often in heraldry, mainly reflecting enemies of the medieval period. The human figure is usually shown fully clothed or, if nearer to nature, is girded around the loins with an extremely uncomfortable "vestment of leaves" described by one English heraldic writer as "vegetable knickers". However, a naked man in all his glory appears in the arms of the Scots baronets Dalyell of the Binns and a breast of sorts, distilling milk, appears in the arms of the English family of Dodge.

Hungarian heraldry affords many instances of the human being in action, whether it be of the bloody kind – slitting the throat of an unfortunate deer or shooting a Turkish soldier – or gentler pursuits such as playing the organ, or reaping corn.

KINGS AND QUEENS

Naturally, the appearance of kings and queens in heraldry is counted to be the highest of all honours. In most cases the monarch commemorated tends to be anonymous, but the Castilian family of de Avila has in its arms an imprisoned king in chains, representing King François I of France, taken prisoner by Don Diego de Avila in 1528 during the Battle of Pavia. The Savoyard family of Amoreto also keeps a Moorish king chained to the chevron in its arms.

The Weldons, Baronets of Rahenderry in Ireland, have the bust of the Virgin Queen, Elizabeth I of England, as their crest. Family records say only that it was given as a mark of distinction by the Queen herself for some great service done to her by a Weldon.

VICTIMS AND VILLAINS

The Spanish family of Miranda commemorates a famous legend on its shield of arms. It bears the busts of five virgins, rescued from rape and murder by Alvar Fernandez de Miranda, while on pilgrimage to Santiago de Compostella. The arms of the city of Lichfield in England record a less favourable fate than that of Alvar's virgins: on old seals of the city council the shield bears "on a landscape proper several martyrs in divers manners massacred."

The English family of Davenport of Capesthorne Hall in Cheshire has what is thought to be a unique crest of a felon's head within the noose from which he is about to be hanged. It refers to the power of life and death, "without delay and without appeal", which the Davenports exercised over vast areas of forest land in north-east England.

HEARTS AND OTHER ORGANS

Human hearts often make their appearance on shields of arms, one forming the central charge in the arms of the Scots family of Douglas. Sir James Douglas was a close companion of King Robert the Bruce of Scotland (1306–29); at the end of his life the king, who had long wished to take part in a Crusade, gained Sir James's promise

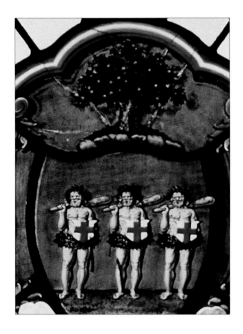

▲ *The wildmen in the arms of the Wood family, traditionally girded with oak leaves.*

▼ *The all too realistic nature of Hungarian arms is borne out here in a grant of 1636.*

▼ *King François I of France stands in chains on the shield of the de Avila family.*

▼ *The virgins saved from a "fate worse than death" by a member of the Miranda family.*

▲ *The crest of the Davenport family of Capesthorne shows an anonymous felon on his way to execution.*

that he would carry the King's embalmed heart to Jerusalem and bury it in the Holy Sephulchre. When the King died in 1329, that is just what Sir James set off to do, but was killed in battle on his journey. Some say he threw King Robert's heart into the fight before following it to certain death. The Douglas family added a red heart to their arms, which was later crowned.

The north Italian family of Colleoni bore three pairs of testicles on their shield. In

▼ *The three pairs of testicles of the Colleoni family, adorning the ceiling of their castle of Malpaga, near Bergamo, north Italy.*

the virile and thoroughly human Middle Ages this was no disgrace, but the dubious gentility of the late 19th century led these vital charges to be described in some ordinaries as three upside-down hearts.

Female genitalia appear on the shield of the medieval Italian family of Conati, but perhaps the most bizarre example of heraldic "vivacity" can be seen on the shield of a Hungarian gentleman, István Várallyay, who in 1599 was granted arms of male sexual organs beneath an arm grasping a mallet. As many Hungarian family arms vividly portray the severed parts of dead Turks, this shield could be taken to represent some particularly unpleasant fate befalling yet another Turkish soldier captured in battle. In truth, however, these particular parts are those of a stallion – Várallyay was a farrier and gelder in the Hungarian army and, being proud of his swiftness and expertise in castrating horses, wished the fact to be recorded in heraldry.

The Indian state of Wankaner has in its arms a representation of the Hindu adoration of the god Shiva, through the veneration of the male phallic symbol of the *lingam*. The arms show Shiva's *trishul*, or trident, wrapped around with snakes, and the round-ended raised stone sculpture that represents the *lingam*, or generative force.

ARMS AND LEGS
Parts of the human body feature regularly in heraldry. The most common are arms or legs. The arms of the Isle of Man are Gules three legs conjoined in fess point in armour proper. They were borne by the ancient kings of Man, and appear as a quartering in the arms of Montagu, Stanley and Murray, all later Lords of Man. The legs probably derive from a Norse symbol for luck introduced by Man's Viking invaders.

A curious human appendage is the wooden leg of the Swede, Per Larsson, who when fighting during the Thirty Years War had his leg amputated. On his eventual ennoblement he took the name Stöltenhielm (*stolt* means "stilt") and a wooden stilt was a main feature in the arms he adopted.

▲ *István Várallyay's shield, with the curious charges that actually celebrate the bearer's profession of farrier and gelder of horses.*

▲ *The arms of the Indian state of Wankaner bring the Hindu worship of Shiva to heraldry.*

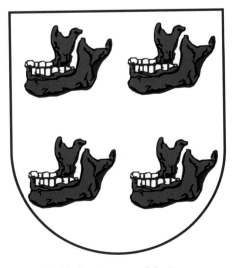

▲ *The highly literal arms of the Portuguese family of Queixada, whose name means simply "jawbone".*

FOWL, FISH AND PLANTS

After animals, the second most popular heraldic charge is birds – most usually the eagle but also less exalted species. Fish of various kinds also sometimes appear, and flowers, trees and even vegetables have also played their part in the heraldic story. Of flowers, the rose and the lily are most commonly met with, and each has a stylized form – the five-petalled heraldic rose and the fleur de lis.

▲ *The stork in its vigilance on the arms of the Hungarian family of Ballint of Técső. If it slept the stone would fall and waken it.*

▼ *The heraldic aviary in the coat of arms of the Barons Arundel shows the imperial eagle behind the shield, the owl as a supporter, and six hirondells (swallows) on the shield.*

HERALDIC BIRDS

If the lion is the king of beasts, the eagle, for medieval heraldic writers, was the queen of birds. From Roman times it was associated with empires, and black eagles were said to be the bravest of all. Both the Byzantine and Holy Roman emperors considered it personal to them.

Many other birds, real, fanciful or fantastic, inhabit the heraldic menagerie, particularly the martlet or *merletten*. The martlet, a swift-like creature, has no feet when depicted in heraldry (and the *merletten* has neither feet nor beak), because it was believed by medieval writers never to land. Such birds were spoken of by Crusaders who had seen them in the Holy Land. The martlet was often given as a heraldic charge to younger sons of the English nobility, as a reminder to "trust to the wings of virtue and merit, and not to their legs, having no land of their own to put their feet on."

The pelican also displays a mixture of fact and fancy. In heraldry it is often depicted using its beak to wound itself in the breast ("vulning"), using the blood it sheds to feed its young. Such a symbol of self-sacrifice is therefore often found in religious arms.

CREATURES OF THE WATER

The dolphin, the most commonly occurring sea creature in heraldry, is classed as a fish by heraldic writers, as is the whale, although both are, of course, mammals. All

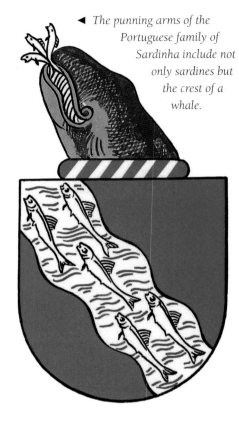

◄ *The punning arms of the Portuguese family of Sardinha include not only sardines but the crest of a whale.*

kinds of fish have appeared as various heraldic charges, but size and ferocity seems to have been foremost in the minds of the medieval heralds. Not surprisingly, therefore, numerous arms can be found bearing the pike, such as the Portuguese family of Lucio, and the Czech town of Dolni Breszov.

▲ *A ferocious and all too realistic pike devours a smaller fish in the arms of the Czech town of Dolni Breszov.*

FLOWERS

Heraldic writers have credited the rose with many properties. It is seen as an emblem of secrecy, being good, soft, and sweet-smelling, but surrounded by evil, signified by its thorns. In medieval England the rose was a popular symbol within the royal family, reaching its zenith during the reigns of the Tudor monarchs. The white rose was a favourite badge of the royal house of York. The red rose of the rival house of Lancaster has a less certain provenance, but it is certain that Henry Tudor (later Henry VII) took it to be the Lancastrian symbol when he united it with the white rose after his marriage to Elizabeth of York in 1486.

The double Tudor rose was a favourite device of Henry VII's son, Henry VIII, and on his marriage to Catherine of Aragon he combined it with the Queen's badge, the pomegranate of Granada. An abundance of roses and pomegranates erupted throughout England, until the eventual divorce of the unhappy couple led to the defacing of any such badge in public places and churches. This must have left Herr Arnold

The fleurs de lis of the French kings are depicted in their crypt in the abbey of St Denis. The shield is encircled by the Order of the Holy Ghost (St Esprit).

Left: the rose and pomegranate charge on the arms of Herr Arnold Bilson – a design he might later have regretted after the divorce of Henry VIII and Catherine of Aragon. Right: The potato flowers of the French town of Ploudaniel.

Bilson, presumably a German merchant in England, in an awkward situation: he had been granted arms charged with a Tudor rose and pomegranate "dimidiated" (halved).

The fleur de lis, the heraldic lily, was associated with the royal house of France long before the advent of heraldry. It is possible that the fleur de lis is a heraldic representation of the flag iris, though one of the many legends surrounding the symbol is that it evolved not from flowers but from three toads, supposedly the arms of Pharamond, King of the Franks in the first half of the 5th century.

As part of the French royal insignia, the fleur de lis can be traced back to the reign of Robert II, "the Pious" (996–1031), son of Hugh Capet. The royal coat of arms, of a blue shield strewn with golden fleurs de lis (semy de lis), made its first appearance during the reign of Louis VIII (1223–6). It is supposed that the number of lilies was reduced to three during the reign of Charles V (1364–80) in honour of the Holy Trinity, although his successor, Charles VI (1380–1422) is known to have used both semy de lis and three fleurs de lis on different occasions.

In modern heraldry, the semy variant is called "France ancient", the three fleurs de lis "France modern". It is possible that the change was an attempt by the French monarchs to distance their arms from their old enemies the English kings, who, starting with Edward III (1327–77) had asserted their claim to the throne of France by quartering the French arms (France ancient) with the lion of England. If such

a ploy was indeed attempted, it did not work, for Henry V of England (1413–22) changed the French quarters in his arms to France modern.

HERALDIC PLANTS

As for other plant life in heraldry, it can lead from the exotic – as with the palm trees in the arms of Maintirano, Malagasy Republic – to the humble, including the potato flower of Ploudaniel, Finistere, France, and the thorn bush (*Spina*) of the Italian family of Malaspina.

The broom plant, or *planta genista* is the emblem of humility, and became the badge adopted by the royal house of Plantagenet. Wheatsheaves, or "garbs", according to Guillaume, were the symbol of plenty and could signify the "harvest of one's hopes". Fruits also symbolized plenty.

The clover leaf, or "trefoil" frequently appears, not least as the shamrock, the plant symbol of Ireland. If a narrow tapering stem is shown projecting from it (or from any other leaf or flower), it is said to be "slipped". Heraldic variants of the trefoil have different numbers of leaves: the quatrefoil (four leaves), cinquefoil (five leaves) and the octofoil (eight leaves), which in England is the mark given to the ninth son.

The arms of the Italian Princes di Massa include the thorn tree of the arms of the Malaspina family.

MONSTERS AND FABULOUS BEASTS

People like to be thrilled by the unknown or strange, so it is not surprising to find in medieval armorials many examples of mythological creatures such as griffins, dragons, centaurs, unicorns and mermaids. Such monsters may have been the product of pure imagination, but it is more likely that they were the result of the need to exaggerate – most medieval heraldists and their patrons having heard at second-, third-, or even fourth-hand of the strange and wonderful creatures discovered in the far-off Indies or Americas.

► *The arms granted to Josef Moise in 1867, during the reign of Emperor Franz Josef of Austria, include a fire-breathing panther.*

▼ *The vibrancy and imagination of medieval heraldry is shown here in the wyvern crest of Sir John Grey de Ruthin.*

We have seen how medieval heraldry treated the relatively familiar lion, putting it into positions that would probably cause the real beast to fall over backwards. The panther was depicted equally fantastically, usually spouting flames from nostrils, mouth and even ears. Medieval bestiaries were the fuel for further heraldic fancies. These works, often wonderfully illustrated, told of cockatrices, bonacons and wyverns: fabulous creatures best encountered only in books and manuscripts. So ferocious were they that often they could turn people to stone on sight, or kill with their breath. Most medieval folk believed these creatures really did exist, and for someone who considered even the next village to be foreign territory, monsters provided just one more reason not to venture far from their own doorsteps.

THE DRAGON

Said to be the greatest of all serpents, the dragon had a scaly body and wings (usually depicted as bat-like). Its head was often horned and tufted, its tail thorny and pointed. It is quite possible that it had its origins in the unearthed fossils of prehistoric beasts. The sheer size of the skeletons that would have been found from time to time throughout the known world, would have been enough to overawe the finder, and real dragons are still alive and well on the island of Komodo off Indonesia, tales of which must have passed between traders many centuries ago.

Dragons lived in caves or deep in the earth's core, where fire was their constant companion; no wonder then that dragons themselves could breathe fire. In British heraldry the dragon is shown with four legs, but this is a late development, for

▲ *A centaur with a bow aiming skywards is an apt charge to appear on a badge for a German Army anti-aircraft unit.*

▲ *The wyvern, a heraldic beast used in England, in earlier times may well have been a dragon.*

▲ *The heraldic griffin is often seen as the guardian of treasure.*

▲ *The bonacon here seems gentle, but its unique defensive technique was all too awesome and far from benign.*

before the 15th century it was usually shown as having just two. In English heraldry the two-legged dragon tends to be called a wyvern or a basilisk, though in the rest of Europe the matter is not so distinct.

THE GRIFFIN

The heraldic monster with the forepart of an eagle and the hindquarters of a lion is called a griffin, or gryphon. Although not quite as popular as the dragon in heraldry, it nevertheless captured the imagination of many noble minds, for the griffin was the guardian of gold and hidden treasure, and was therefore a creature to be met on many a medieval quest.

▲ *The unicorn on the arms of the Polish noble tribe of Boncza is one of the few mythical beasts in Polish heraldry.*

In British heraldry a so-called male griffin is shown without wings, its body covered in tufts of formidable spikes, which are usually of a different colour to the rest of its body. Confusingly, the ordinary griffin is also normally depicted as having male sexual organs: just what a female griffin should look like is not made clear by heraldic writers. In English heraldry the griffin when in the rampant position is described as being "segreant".

THE UNICORN

Many a medieval prince kept a so-called unicorn's horn in his collection of curios, though in reality this was likely to be the tusk of a narwhal. The subject of many noble fantasies and legends, the unicorn is considered by many to be the most beautiful creature in the heraldic menagerie. In effect it is part horse, part heraldic antelope, with a large twisting horn or tusk issuing from its forehead. It is also depicted as having a lion's tail and a little tuft of hairs under its chin. So pure a creature is the unicorn that it is often entirely white, apart from its horn, tufts, mane and hooves, which are gold. When regally collared and chained, unicorns are the supporters beloved of the Scots monarchs.

In medieval romances, tales were told of how the usually untameable unicorn would befriend a gentle damsel of noble birth whom it sensed to be a virgin. When the noble creature had found such a lady it would lay its head in her lap and go to sleep. It was only at such a moment that hunters could steal in and capture or kill this wonderful prey.

The purity of both the unicorn and virgin was made much of by medieval writers, who compared the two symbols to Christ and the Virgin Mary. Because of this sacred connection some heraldic authors of the medieval period considered that the unicorn should not be sullied by placing its image on shield or crest. However, by the 16th century it had become a popular charge in heraldry all over Europe, appearing on shields as far apart as Poland, where it is borne by the Herb (clan or tribe) of Boncza, and in Italy by the Bardi family of Florence.

▲ *An exotic flavour is given to the ancient theme of the mermaid in the arms of Mouila in the Gabon, where a sirene was said to haunt the local river luring men to her lair.*

OTHER BEASTS

Like the salamander, depicted as a lizard surrounded by flames, the phoenix often appears in the arms of towns and cities that have been rebuilt after destruction in war. Classical writers asserted that only one phoenix existed at a time, and lived for 500 years. Knowing its end to be near, it made a nest that the sun's rays ignited, frying the poor bird. Out of the embers came its successor.

A creature peculiar to English heraldry is the bonacon. Somewhat like a bull with blunted horns that were turned inwards, the bonacon was said to defend itself by emitting burning excreta which could cover an enormous area.

MARINE MONSTERS

The mermaid was busy luring sailors to various fates, happy or decidedly nasty, from earliest times. Said to be half woman, half fish, she probably arose from sailors' sightings of the dugong or sea-cow.

The sirene seems to be a curious cousin of the mermaid with two tails. A version is found in the arms designed in the late 20th century for the commune of Mouila in the Gabon. Said to appear from time to time to claim a local man for her husband, the sirene displays two splendid scarlet tails. The white sister of Mouila's sirene appears in the arms of several European families, including the Amari of Sicily.

INANIMATE CHARGES

Heraldry has always made full and free use of every kind of object, and coats of arms reflect life's events from the cradle to the grave. The arms of the French town of St Germain-en-Laye include a very grand baby's cradle that also bears the date – 5 September 1638 – on which the future Louis XIV was born. At the other extreme, the last resting place of one of the earliest humans, found during mining activities in northern Rhodesia (now Zimbabwe), is suggested by a skull in the arms of Broken Hill, granted in 1954. A complete skeleton in a somewhat reflective pose in the civic arms of Londonderry, Northern Ireland, recalls the unhappy fate of a local nobleman, Walter de Burgo, who was starved to death in a dungeon on the orders of one of his own family members.

CLOTHING AND ACCESSORIES

All kinds of dress can be met with, from the mundane (the breeches in the arms of the family of Van Abbenbroek from Zeeland) to the curious (a French wife's hood, the heraldic badge of the English 16th-century nobleman Lord Ferrers). As early as the 14th century, fashion was appearing on the nobleman's shield. The lady's sleeve or "maunch", which had a pendulous pocket to house the owner's prayer book or missal, was a popular charge in English and French heraldry throughout the late medieval period.

A medieval lady might well also have treasured a necklace of Baltic amber, such

▲ From the cradle – Louis XIV of France's birth is remembered in the arms of the town of St Germain-en-Laye.

▲ To the grave – a rather bored skeleton of Walter de Burgo in the arms of the city of Londonderry, Northern Ireland.

▲ A pair of sandals is the charge for the Spanish family of Abarca.

▲ The buildings of the gentry – three of the cotes that they kept their doves in, the punning arms of the English family of Sapcote.

▲ The way we earn our bread – the sewing machine in the arms of Clydebank, Scotland, home of Singer sewing machines.

▲ The inventor, proud of his works – the corrugated boiler flue that made a fortune for Samson Fox of Harrogate.

as the one found in the arms of the Lithuanian coastal resort of Palanga, where lumps of the fossilized resin are often washed up on the beaches.

BUILDINGS AND WORK

Fortresses and bridges appear on shields, as do homes, from the stone building in the arms of the town of Frontenhausen, Bavaria, to the Inuit igloo that forms the crest of the Territory of Nunuvut, Canada. Even the turrets of Indian homes, or *gonkhs*, find their way on to the arms of Halvad Dhrangadhra in Gujarat. A church features in the punning arms of the Asturian family of Iglesia.

The workplace, whether it be the coal mine of the community of Bütten (in the arms of Landkreis Peine, Westphalia) or a

▲ *The food we eat – the sugar loaves of Waghausel, Landkreis Karlsruhe, Germany, appear here in the trademark of the town's sugar refinery.*

▲ *The warrior chef – the cheese grater and noodle flattener crest of the Master of the Kitchens to the Holy Roman Emperor.*

sewing machine made in a factory at Burgh of Clydebank, Scotland shows that heraldry can reflect the lifestyle of the worker just as well as that of a medieval knight. Whether the corrugated boiler flue of Samson Fox of Harrogate, England or the section of bracing in the arms of the Bossom baronets (also English) constitute good heraldic charges, is open to dispute.

Both knight and motorway magnate need to eat, and the kitchen has often figured in heraldic imagination, sometimes turning the most mundane objects into comical or bizarre charges. Even the proverbial kitchen sink probably features on a shield somewhere – certainly the table does. Charges taken from the kitchen include the sugar loaf of Waghausel, Landkreis Karlsruhe, Germany; the standing dishes in the punning arms of the English family of Standish; a trivet (Trivet of Cornwall); and a kettle hanger for the town of Zwijndrecht in the Netherlands. So important was the medieval kitchen in the running of a noble or royal household that the Master of the Kitchens to the Holy Roman Emperor was afforded his own very distinctive crest – a cheese grater and a noodle flattener.

TRANSPORT

In the last two centuries the railway has cut its way across the heraldic shields of towns from Swindon in England to Kaisiadorys in Lithuania. The former has a conventional locomotive of the late 19th century (there was much correspondence between the town council and the College of Arms in London over the exact make of the locomotive), while in the arms of the latter, four stylized silver steeds, streaming steam and smoke, pass back and forth across a black shield to represent the two major railways running through the town.

Cars also found their way on to the proud shields of factory towns such as Koprovince in the Czech Republic, the home of the first Czech car, the President, which rolled off the production line in 1897. Air travel was to make its mark on shields from the early 20th century onwards, a startling example being found in the arms of the commune of Sandweiler

▲ *The four rather dashing stylized iron horses of Kaisiadorys, Lithuania.*

▼ *The President car on the arms of Koprovince in the Czech Republic.*

▲ *A jet lands on the runway of the airport at Sandweiler, Luxembourg, giving traditional heraldic ordinaries a modern flavour.*

▲ *The arms of Mary, Duchess of Bedford, were drawn up and insisted upon by her husband, in spite of the heralds' disapproval.*

in Luxembourg. Sandweiler is home to Luxembourg's international airport, so a passenger jet lands on an intersection of runways in the arms.

One aircraft that had rather a bumpy journey through the heraldic skies, made its maiden flight in the unofficial arms of Mary, wife of the 11th Duke of Bedford. The Duchess was a well-known lady aviator in the 1930s and her husband wished the College of Arms to record the fact in a

grant of arms to his wife, but the heralds would not sanction the design, which the Duke had himself helped to create, including the Duchess's favourite plane, the Spider. This seems not to have bothered His Grace one jot: he claimed that his family, the Russells, had long ago used arms not granted by any herald, and what was done in the past was good enough for his dear wife in her own time.

Even the parachute has been used as a heraldic charge, most notably in the arms of Ste Mère-Eglise in Normandy, commemorating the day in 1944 when the paratroopers of the US Army's 101st Airborne Division landed in and around the town's church – one man even found himself draped across the church tower, an event memorably depicted in the film *The Longest Day*.

SPORTS AND GAMES

Heraldry can also catalogue the lighter side of life, such as the tennis-playing youths in the arms of the Tosetti family of Massiola, northern Italy. In Britain where the weather is not so propitious for outdoor sports, board games find their way on to the heraldic shield, as in the arms of

the Pegrez family with its backgammon boards, and the arms of the Matthias family of Lamphey in Pembrokeshire: Gules on each of three dice in perspective Argent 11 ogresses six in front three on the sinister two on top.

▲ *A tennis match in which, for reasons unknown, the players are not wearing any clothes, features in the arms of the north Italian family of Tosetti.*

▼ *Three backgammon boards appear in the arms of the English family of Pegrez.*

◄ *The arms of the French village of Ste Mère-Eglise in Normandy commemorate the landing of American paratroopers at the church, during the liberation of the region from Germany in 1944.*

▲ A skiing warrior appears in the arms of the town of Lillehammer, Norway.

▲ Sir George Edwards' arms feature blue skies and Concordes for a life in aviation.

▲ The town of Spa in Belgium, famous for its waters, has the old spa as its arms.

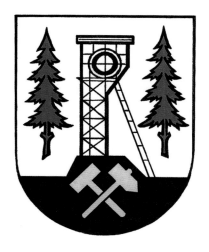

▲ The local coal mine appears in the arms of Bülten in Landkreis Peine, Germany.

▲ Two towns in Germany, Oerlese and...

▲ ...Rietze, maintain a heraldic link with the traditional practices of local farming.

▲ The sails of the ships in the arms of the Scottish Royal Burgh of Elie and Earlsferry are charged with the arms of local lords.

▲ The ship, star and crescent in the arms of the Danish port of Nörresundby, originally on a seal, were adapted to a shield.

▲ A detailed depiction of an oared 18th-century sailing ship adorns the shield of the Crimean port of Kostroma.

PUNNING HERALDRY

The richness of heraldic imagery and imagination is nowhere more apparent than in those arms that have been devised as a play on the bearer's name. Punning or, as it is known in Britain, "canting" heraldry, can account for almost half the designs of some nations' heraldry.

Although the great majority of arms dating from the early days of heraldry were of a simple geometric nature, the heraldic imagination at work in the arms of León and Castile (which have always featured a lion and a castle) is a good example of the simplicity of the practice.

A PLAY ON WORDS

The motto of the Scudamores is *Scuto amore divinis* ("The shield of divine love"): the shield bears a gold field with a red cross patty fitchy. The Montagus (or Montacutes) bear three fusils (elongated lozenges) conjoined in fess, the tops of which are supposed to suggest the tops of mountains or *mons acutus*. The prize for the most tortuous wordplay must probably go to the arms of the powerful Mortimer family, whose arms include blue and gold bars with a white escutcheon over all. The blue represents the skies of

► *The quartered arms of Castile and León in Toledo Cathedral, 16th century, epitomize the simplicity of punning or canting.*

▲ *The three bear's paws of Trebarefoote.*

▲ *The three hands of Tremayne.*

▲ *The Scudamore shield of divine love.*

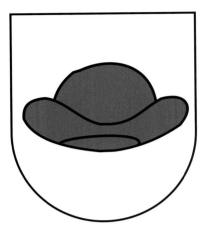

▲ *The family arms of Rotenhuet (red hat) of Silesia.*

▲ *The arms of the Rosensparre (rose chevron) family of Denmark.*

▲ *The family arms of Swinhufvud (swine head) of Sweden.*

the Holy Land, the gold its sands, while the escutcheon is said to represent the Dead Sea or *mortuo maris*.

In Cornwall, the local placenames offer plenty of opportunities for good puns on the number three through their common prefix "Tre". Trebarefoote has Sable a chevron between three bear's gambs (feet) erect and erased Or, and Tremayne has Gules three dexter arms conjoined at the shoulders and flexed in triangle Or, fists clenched Argent.

One of the most delightful examples has survived through the skill and imagination of the late medieval English stonemason who, asked to fashion the crest of a member of the Mordaunt family for a tomb in Northamptonshire, produced a grinning Moor showing all his teeth – literally "Moor's dents". A modern-day equivalent is the former Aeroplane and Armaments

▼ *The Moor shows off his splendid set of teeth in the Mordaunt crest.*

Experimental Establishment based at Boscombe Down in England. The English heralds came up with the local bird, a bustard, standing in a coombe (valley) on a down. That left the "Bos" which was provided by pinning the poor bustard's wing with the boss from a horse's bridle.

A EUROPEAN TRADITION

Medieval wordplay ranges from the commonplace to the curious. The Zurich armorial roll, held in the Swiss National Museum, supplies many splendid examples of punning German arms from the early 14th century. The Rand family arms are Sable a turnip Proper leaved Vert (*Rande* is German for "turnip"). The von Helfensteins of Swabia have Gules on a quadruple mount Or, an elephant statant Argent and as the Old German word for "beggar" is *betler*, the Betler family arms are Argent a beggar habited in Sable, his

shoes Or, on his shoulder a knapsack of the field, suspended by a cord Gules, a pilgrim's staff in his sinister hand, and in his dexter a begging bowl, both of the last.

Scandinavian heraldry has a long history of punning, and has made excellent use of the device. The medieval period produced the simple arms of the Swedish noble families of Sparre – Azure a chevron Or (*sparre* is a roof span, or chevron) – and Swinhufvud: Azure a boar's head couped Or (*swinhuf* meaning swine's head).

Probably the most innovative of modern punning heraldry emerged in Finland in the latter half of the 20th century. A good example is the arms of the municipality of Aanekoski, which translates from the local dialect as "sounding river" (*ääni* means "voice" and *koski*, "rapids"): Sable on a bend wavy Argent three horns stringed Gules.

▲ *The bustard stands in his coombe.*

▲ *The sounding rapids of Aanekoski, Finland.*

MESSAGES AND DECLARATIONS

It might seem that once the design of a shield had been settled it would never change. On the medieval battlefield or tourney ground this would have been true, but heraldry is a great adaptor and certain traits have crept in over the centuries that would not have been used by a 13th-century knight. Above all, heraldry was the plaything of the European aristocracy, and arms could be a useful way of accentuating their owner's place in that closely knit class. Coronets of rank started to appear in the 15th century, and special marks of favour granted by a grateful monarch could be thrust in the faces of rivals by displaying them in a coat of arms. Relationships to other families through marriage could be indicated by placing the two sets of arms together. In England if a wife had no brothers she was deemed a heraldic heiress, her children having equal right to display her father's and mother's arms on heraldic quarters, and as other generations married heiresses, so the original arms could be pushed into one corner of the shield by other symbols.

◄ *The arms of the Princes Bagration of Russia, with the princely mantle and crown.*

AUGMENTATION OF ARMS

Rulers have always availed themselves of orders and decorations to reward those who have served their country, but there is another way for a grateful ruler to thank the patriot or the peacemaker – by the augmentation of armorial bearings. Augmentations are additions to arms that in some way reflect the gratitude of the donor. They are added either by "honour"– when the grantee has performed deeds of merit – or by "grace", whereby the sovereign grants part of his or her arms to a relative. It cannot be said that Henry VIII did much for his wives, but he did give augmentations of grace to the families of three of them.

The augmentation is often a charge from the donor's own arms, or a new coat in the form of a quartering. In the latter case (in British heraldry) the new quarter of augmentation takes first place, with the old arms moving into the second quarter. Crests and supporters may also be given as augmentation. In Britain, an augmentation takes the form of a new grant from either the College of Arms (England and Wales) or Lord Lyon (Scotland), which tends to include a special citation mentioning the reason for the augmentation.

▼ Colonel Carlos' royal companion in the branches of an oak tree is commemorated in the family arms.

▲ Dr Lake bravely rides on in the crest of augmentation, while his 16 wounds are on the 1st quarter to the family arms.

AUGMENTATIONS OF CHARLES II

The reason for the granting of augmentations of honour is neatly summed up in the words of the English King Charles II who, after the Civil War, issued a warrant to Sir Edward Walker, Garter King of Arms, to grant "unto any person of eminent quality, fidelity and extraordinary merit that shall desire it, such augmentation of any of our Royal Badges to be added unto his Armes, as you shall judge most proper to testify the same".

Among the augmentations that Sir Edward granted, several referred to Charles II's escape after the defeat of the Royalist forces at Worcester in 1651, in which he was aided by loyal friends, Early in his escape, the King and his companion Colonel Careless evaded their pursuers by hiding in an oak tree at Boscobel House. This episode was remembered in augmentations to Colonel William Carlos (as his name was now) and the Penderel brothers, tenants of Boscobel. Both families received a full grant of arms which included an oak tree surmounted of a fess charged with three crowns.

Among other extraordinary episodes of the King's flight was riding pillion on the bay horse of Mistress Jane Lane, disguised

as a tenant's son. Not only were the Lanes granted a canton of the royal arms of England, they were also later granted a crest of augmentation: Out of a wreath Or and Azure a demi horse Strawberrie colour, bridled Sable, bitted and garnished Or, supporting an imperial crown Gold.

During the English Civil War an augmentation was granted to Dr Edward Lake for his valour at the Battle of Edgehill in 1642 when he was wounded no less than 16 times, one of which rendered his left arm useless. He was then said to have taken his horse's reins in his teeth, an action that is recorded in the crest of augmentation. All 16 wounds are also remembered in the coat of augmentation, which took the first quarter of his arms. This shows a dexter arm in armour grasping a sword, from which flies a flag of St George. The cross is charged with a lion

▲ The arms of Abensberg, Bavaria (left), were later augmented with swords (right) for the town's help in the Napoleonic wars.

▼ Drake's ship does its balancing act upon the globe of his extravagant arms.

▲ *The arms of concession to Christopher Columbus; the original family arms are in the base of the shield.*

passant guardant from the royal arms, and in each quarter of the flag are four red escutcheons, one for each wound.

VOYAGES OF EXPLORATION

The late medieval period saw the monarchs of Europe vie with each other in gaining for themselves the wealth of the wider world. They were aided by professional sailors who put their lives and ships at risk in return for a small part of the riches and prestige they might present to their sovereign, but all too often these great voyagers received shabby compensation for their efforts. They could, however, receive heraldic recognition. The shield borne by the descendants of Christopher Columbus contains four separate quarters as augmentations, the original family arms being relegated, almost as an afterthought, to a point in the base of the shield. A crest of the royal orb, a rare distinction in Spanish heraldry, was also given together with the motto:

A *Castillion y Leon, nuevo munda, dio Colon,* "To Castile and León, the new world was given by Colón".

Another explorer, Vasco da Gama, of Portugal, received the ancient shield of arms of Portugal as an augmentation: Argent five escutcheons in cross Azure each charged with five plates. He was also given the crest of a demi man dressed "a l'Indienne" holding a shield of the augmented arms and a branch of cinnamon, all evoking his epic voyage to India and the Spice Islands.

The English adventurer, Sir Francis Drake, was said to have been using the arms of another Devon family of the same name, whose head complained to Elizabeth I, calling the famous explorer an upstart. The Queen retorted that she would give Sir Francis arms which would far outshine those of his namesake. Those arms, Sable a fess wavy between two estoiles irradiated Argent, neatly sum up his voyages between the North and South Poles. The crest is a case of paper heraldry and could never be used on any helmet. Various depictions show a ship on top of a globe being guided by a hand from clouds, holding a golden cord; above the clouds a scroll with the motto *Auxilio divino* ("By divine aid"). The blazon of the crest also includes "in the ship a dragon Gules regarding the hand".

FRENCH AUGMENTATIONS

The French monarchs were not usually forthcoming with granting any augmentations, but they could not avoid acknowledging the part played by Joan of Arc in the eventual eviction of the English. In 1429, Charles VII granted to Joan's family a simple but splendid shield

▲ *Vasco da Gama's voyages to the Spice Islands are remembered in his crest of concession (augmentation).*

▲ *A diplomatic alliance remembered heraldically – the viper of the Viscontis is augmented by the fleurs de lis of France.*

of a blue field charged with an erect sword supporting the French crown and two fleurs de lis in fess. These arms recall an account by the chronicler, Holinshed, that Joan wielded a sword "With five floure delices graven on both sides", and although there is no evidence to suggest Joan used the arms, they were used by the descendants of her brothers, upon whom Charles VII conferred the name Du Lys.

Both the Viscontis of Milan and the Medicis of Florence could be said to have been awarded augmentations "of grace" by French monarchs. In 1395 Charles VI

▼ *The arms of Joan of Arc's brothers' descendants, her sword upholding the crown.*

▲ *Heraldry in 3D: in the arms of the Medicis the topmost roundel is charged with the fleurs de lis of France.*

conceded by special diploma to Gian Galeazzo Visconti the right to quarter the arms of France (ancient) within a double border the external Gules the internal Argent. The Medici arms are thought to include a pun on their name, the red roundels in the shield possibly being pills (*palle*) handed out by doctors (*medici*). In 1465 Louis XI granted the Medicis the right to replace the top roundel with a blue one charged with three gold fleurs de lis.

RALLYING TO ARMS

The arms of many Polish families evolved on the battlefield, and they offer some unusual examples of augmentation. In 1386 the neighbouring states of Poland and Lithuania were joined through the marriage of the daughter of the last Polish king of the Piast dynasty to Grand Duke Jagiello of Lithuania. The Polish arms (a white eagle on a red field) were afterwards quartered with Lithuania's charging knight.

Under the Jagiellon dynasty, if a man was raised to nobility through valour, it became the custom to give him a shield charged with an arm in armour holding a sword. This coat was known as the "Pogonia". Later Polish kings – notably those of the Vasa dynasty – would grant foreigners, such as ambassadors, who had offered good service to the state, part of the Polish eagle as an augmentation. (Venetian ambassadors to London also managed to obtain augmentations to their arms, and several examples are extant which bear in their design the lion passant guardant Or of the English sovereign.)

The arms of Moravia, Azure an eagle displayed chequy Argent and Gules, have long been considered one of the most beautiful in medieval heraldry. When the Moravians came to the aid of the Holy Roman Emperor Frederick III (1440–93) he granted them the right to change the white chequers of the eagle to gold. In 1848, the year of revolution, Moravians supporting the Czech independence movement pledged support to the ancient eagle with white and red chequers, while German-speaking Moravians used the augmented gold and red chequered bird as their symbol.

Many Russian noble arms include the ciphers of sovereigns and charges taken from the arms of the Romanov emperors, but surely the most augmented arms of all must be those of Count Alexander Suvorov-Rymniksky, commander of the Russian Armies, whose brilliant strategies helped to bring about the eventual defeat of Napoleon. As commander-in-chief of the Russo-Austrian Army during the Second Coalition, he drove the French out of northern Italy in 1799 and was created Prince Italiysky. He had also previously defeated a Turkish force on the banks of the River Rymnik in Turkey in 1789. The augmentations to his arms included a "rendering of the map of Italy", an escutcheon bearing the name of Emperor Paul I, and two lightning bolts issuing from thunderclouds striking a crescent reversed above a river in bend inscribed *R Rymnik*. His services to the Russian nation were commemorated not only by an imperial decoration, but also by the Soviet Union.

▲ *The proud eagle of Moravia sports its distinctive golden chequers.*

▶ *Count Torelli's arms are augmented not only with the Visconti viper but also with his master's personal impresa and motto.*

The German emperors made full and free use of the Prussian eagle (often as supporters) in augmentations to those who had assisted in their rise to imperial power in the 19th century. Alexander von Schleinitz, Prussian Foreign Minister, received supporters to his arms of two Prussian eagles charged on the breast with the arms of Hohenzollern. Otto, Prince Bismarck, who brought about German unification, was granted a Prussian (black) and a Brandenburg (red) eagle as supporters: they supported two armorial bearings, those of Alsace and Lorraine, the territories regained from France in 1870–1.

LATER AUGMENTATIONS

In the late 18th and early 19th centuries heraldry in most countries was in a state of decay, or rather decadence. The augmentations granted to the military and

naval heros of Britain were typical of the period, with battle scenes, bombardments, storming of forts and "casts of thousands", or medals with inscriptions and too detailed to be legible. The arms of Rear Admiral Sir Charles Brisbane included a

chief "thereon on waves of the sea a ship of war under sail between two forts, the guns firing and on the battlements the Dutch flag all proper". Colonel James Stevenson-Barnes had a canton charged with his gold cross and the Portuguese Order of the Tower and Sword; his arms also included a chief bearing a curtain of fortification and the name *St Sebastian*.

Medals and decorations remained in vogue as augmentations to arms well into the 20th century. On 2 May 1918 the Finnish city of Vaasa was informed that: "To commemorate the time when Vaasa as the temporary capital was the heart of the liberation of Finland [from Russia], the Senate have decided to give the City the right to add the Cross of Liberty to its coat of arms." Another Finnish city, Mikkeli, housed the headquarters of Marshal Mannerheim's army, and on 21 December 1944 the medal of the Cross of Liberty was suspended from its shield. This was the second augmentation given to Mikkeli, in 1942 it was granted a pair of crossed marshal's batons.

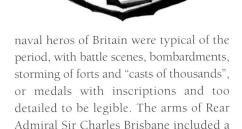

▼ *One of three shield designs supplied by the heraldic artist to the Vaasa authorities for consideration. Here the augmentation is simply placed on the heraldic charge.*

▼ *Another suggestion put before the committee makes the augmentation of the cross more prominent.*

▼ *In this suggestion the charge becomes secondary as the augmentation takes pride of place with the star of the order.*

ABATEMENTS AND DEGRADATIONS

Augmentations were marks of honour, given in the main to the strong and heroic, those who had rendered great service to their sovereign and their nation. But military men can also go astray. They may contravene the code of chivalry, or even betray their own country. What then should become of such traitors, debauchees, boasters and other miscreants? For the treacherous knight, his class had a most terrible ceremony – "the degradation from knighthood".

KNIGHTS AND KNAVES

John Selden, in his work *Titles of Honour* (1614), describes the case of Sir Andrew de Harclay, Earl of Carlisle, who in the 16th year of the reign of Edward II (1307–27) was condemned as a traitor,

▲ *The reversed royal arms of Portugal on the shield of Castello-Rodrigo are a rare case of an abatement put into practice.*

having secretly treated with the Scots against the King's favourite, Hugh Le Despenser. Edward was told of Harclay's doings and ordered the Earl's immediate apprehension. Harclay was seized at Carlisle and brought against a court of his peers. The Earl was found guilty, and sentence was pronounced against him that the sword (which he had received from the King "to defend his Lord" and with which he had been made Earl) should be taken from him, and his gilt spurs hacked from his heels by a "knave", after which the Earl's sword was to be broken over his head. The Earl was divested of his tabard, his hood, his coat and his "girdle". When this was done Sir Anthony Lucy (one of the judges) said to the Earl "Andrew, now art thou no knight but thou art a knave."

Selden also quotes the case of Sir Ralfe Grey, a Knight of the Bath who was

◄ *The defaced arms of Henry Courtenay, Marquess of Exeter, attainted and executed in 1539 after falling foul of King Henry VIII.*

▼ *The arms of Plommenfelt, a Swedish nobleman. His arms were erased after he was declared "dead" in punishment for slandering the Swedish king.*

degraded from knighthood. The Constable of England, being empowered to sit in judgement, said to the accused, "The King has ordained that thou should have had thy spurs stricken off by the hard heels, by the hand of the Master Cooke… and here thou mayest see, the Kings of Armes, and Heralds and thine own proper coat of armes which they should teare off thy bodie, and so shouldst thou as well be degraded of the Worship, Noblenesse and Armes, as of thy Order of Knighthood."

The Constable had with him another coat of arms, reversed (upside-down) as a sign of dishonour, which should have been worn by Sir Ralfe on his way to the place of execution, but it seems that he was spared this further token of degradation as the King remembered the good service done by the former knight's grandfather to the King's "Most Noble Predecessors".

In the case of knights of certain orders, the Garter included, further punishment could be expected. In addition to the measures taken during the service of degradation, their trappings of knighthood – targe, helm and crest – were to be torn down from their place in the chapel of the order, and literally kicked out into a nearby ditch; the knight's shield was also broken in pieces. In the Catholic Church a similar ceremony of defrocking was ordained as the most serious penalty reserved for clergy who had broken ecclesiastical laws.

CIVIC BETRAYALS
The 17th-century heraldist John Guillim cited the case of Sir Aimery of Pavia, a Lombard, an unworthy Captain of Calais in the time of Edward III (1327–77), who sold the town to the enemy for 20,000 crowns. Guillim described Sir Aimery's arms as "Light blue, four mullets yellow, two in fess, as many in the chief, reversed (upside-down)".

In Portugal, the town of Castello-Rodrigo was made to bear a shield charged with the arms of Portugal reversed, because the townsfolk had closed the gates on a rival claimant to the Portuguese throne who subsequently proved victorious. This is one of the very few cases of an abatement put into practice.

MARKS OF ABATEMENT
Various English books on heraldry include certain marks of dishonour that have been termed "abatements". They employ charges and stains – the lesser and rare colours tenny (tawny or orange) and sanguine (blood red) – borne together in a fashion otherwise uncommon in heraldry. The sixth edition of John Guillim's monumental work *A Display of Heraldry* (1724), "improved" by Sir George Mackenzie, listed the abatements. They are illustrated below. Most of these abatements were probably the doodlings of some herald in the Tudor period. The English herald J. P. Brooke-Little, in his foreword to his revison of Boutell's *Heraldry* (1970), asserted that "there is no such thing as a mark of dishonour in English heraldry." Nor does such a system exist anywhere else.

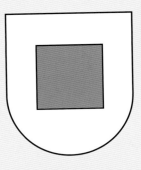

▲ A delf tenny: he who revokes his own challenge.

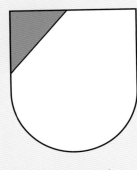

▲ Argent a point dexter parted tenny: a boaster of martial acts.

▲ Or a point in point sanguine: effeminacy.

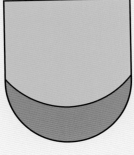

▲ Or a point champaine tenny: one who kills a prisoner after surrender.

▲ Argent a gore sinister tenny: a coward to his enemy.

▲ Or a plain point sanguine: a liar.

◀ A combination of two marks of abatement: Argent a gusset sinister sanguine: he who is "devoted too much to the smock", or womanizing, and Argent a gusset dexter sanguine: a man too fond of drink. If guilty of both, the man should bear both gussets, as here.

▲ The shield reversed: a traitor, also denotes death.

FANTASTICAL ARMS

Heraldry has long been seen as an accoutrement of the high-born, both present and past. From the 15th to the 17th centuries, heraldic writers increasingly sought to bestow arms on those of high rank in history and legend. Rulers, saints, biblical characters and legendary figures both good and bad, were assumed to have borne arms, as their like did in more recent times. No matter that documentary evidence was at the least scant, the heraldic writers felt that it was their duty to invent retrospective arms for those who were thought to be worthy of them.

HOLY ARMS

The holy Trinity – God the Father, Son and Holy Ghost – was represented in the "Arms of the Faith", the three joined in one upon the shield. The symbols of the Passion can often be found on a series of shields displayed in parish churches throughout Europe. The three kings, or wise men, who

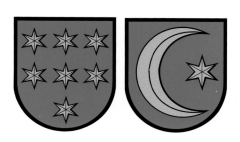

▲ ▼ *Attributed arms for the three wise men: Casper (above left), Balthasar (above right) and Melchior (below).*

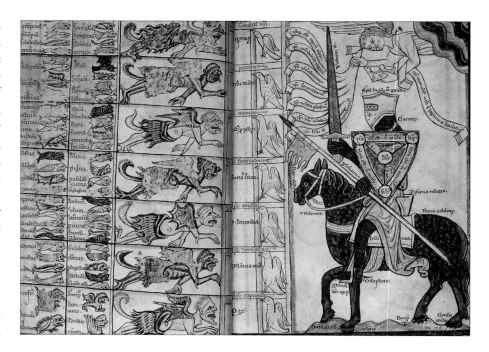

visited the Christ child also had arms attributed to them by medieval heraldists. As for Satan, the Prince of Darkness, he also held a rank of sorts and was therefore afforded arms in medieval manuscripts: a shield with frogs and a fess accompanied him as he dragged the souls of fallen knights from the field down into hell.

In India, the arms of various Hindu gods, in particular Hanuman the monkey god, appear in the arms of several states.

▼ *The charge attributed to Hector, champion of Troy, and one of the Nine Worthies thought to deserve posthumous arms.*

▲ *A Christian knight, his shield charged with the attributed arms of the holy Trinity, rides out to fight vice and heresy, shown here in the form of devils, in a 13th-century illuminated manuscript.*

THE NINE WORTHIES

Many allegorical tales of the medieval period concerned the Nine Worthies of the World, a group composed of those who were believed to have been the greatest warriors of history. Their characters were especially appealing to the writers of the early Renaissance, who attempted to recreate their heroic feats.

Three of the Worthies were outstanding commanders of the classical world: Hector of Troy, Julius Caesar and Alexander the Great; three were biblical heroes of the Old Testament, Joshua, Judas Maccabeus and David; and three were European Christian warriors, King Arthur of the Britons, King Charlemagne of France, and Godfrey de Bouillon, the leader of the First Crusade. The Worthies of this splendid band were notable rulers and generals, men to be feared and followed, and would therefore surely all have merited arms. Consequently, armorial bearings were devised for all nine. The arms given to the Worthies by heraldic

▼ *The arms of the princes Bagration of Russia, whose ancestral claims are declared with King David's harp, and the sling he used to slay Goliath.*

▲ *Four Saxon kings, who lived long before heraldry was established, are depicted with attributed arms in the quarters of this stained-glass shield at Capesthorne Hall, Cheshire, England.*

writers of the 16th and 17th centuries reflected the attributes and character generally attributed to each man. Ferocity, bravura, steadfastness and mercy naturally featured strongly. Many of their arms therefore bear lions in various attitudes, and creatures such as wyverns, dragons and double-headed eagles. The Jewish heroes bore symbols usually associated with the Tribes of Israel.

OTHER ATTRIBUTED ARMS

Some families still extant today make use of arms attributed to supposed early ancestors of theirs. The English family of Temple quarters in its arms Or an eagle displayed Sable attributed to Leofric, Earl of Mercia, who was the husband of the more famous Lady Godiva. However, this claim to fame in family history is mundane compared to that of the Russian Princes Bagration, who claim descent from King David of the Jews,

◄ *A spirited depiction in Celtic style of arms attributed to King Arthur by the Cornish artist Dennis Ivall.*

and bear in their arms his harp, and the sling and stone with which he slew Goliath. Other Russian princely families bear in their arms the figure of the Archangel Gabriel, from whom they claim descent.

Men such as King David, Julius Caesar or Leofric, Earl of Mercia, all obviously lived long before heraldry was invented. The shields they were given posthumously are therefore called "attributed arms". Some of the most famous arms are those attributed to King Arthur and his Knights of the Round Table, and these have been extensively used in artistic depictions of the Arthurian legends from medieval times up to the pre-Raphaelites.

King Arthur has at least three separate shields of arms attributed to him, including Azure three crowns in pale Or, and Vert a cross Argent in the first quarter a figure of the Virgin holding the Christ Child Or. Arthur's first knight and champion, Sir Lancelot du Lac was given Argent three bendlets Gules, and Sir Perceval bore a shield Purpure semy of plain crosslets Or.

ALLIANCES

The joy of heraldry is that it can, by colours and symbols, make an instant visual statement in the most splendid manner, and over the centuries its supporters adapted it to suit their own needs. By the late 15th century, its purpose on the battlefield was in the main lost (due to the discourteous nature of gunfire and to the pride of the wearer in his splendid new "alwyte" armour), but heraldry found other uses. As far back as the 13th century, arms were being married to others to symbolize family ties through marriage, and that was not all they could express. Individuals of knightly rank could, and indeed did, make use of their arms to express ties of friendship and devotion, passion or duty.

EXPRESSIONS OF UNITY

In times gone by, kings would set their arms alongside those of other rulers to assert that they were part of an international élite without equal, and according to medieval thought it was a position they maintained when they were elevated to heaven, where a special "celestial palace" was reserved for the souls of deceased royalty. At the other end of the heraldic

▶ *The unity of marriage: heraldry is utilized in a 15th-century manuscript that shows Isabeau of Bavaria arriving in Paris for her marriage to Charles VI of France, with their impaled arms much in evidence.*

hierarchy, the local landowner could also choose to decorate his castle or manor house with the arms of his equals in the locality. A charming example can still be seen at the former home of the Fairfax family at Gilling Castle in Yorkshire, England. The castle's Great Chamber was decorated in the Elizabethan period with a frieze of

▲ *As these crusading knights gather for their voyage to the holy land their arms are proudly displayed on shields and banners.*

painted trees, from which hang the shields of all the landowning families that governed the local administrative districts, or "wapentakes".

▲ One use of heraldry was to extol the merits of feudalism. In the Armorial General, 14th century, the arms of the King of England are followed by those of his vassals.

Elsewhere the comradeship in arms of various knights was recorded less formally. Graffiti is by no means a product of the modern age: witness the crudely etched shields, crests and signatures scratched into the stone and plaster of the Sanctuary of the Nativity in Bethlehem some seven centuries ago by Crusaders, who were probably part of a contingent of knights from Flanders.

▲ Alliances of brotherhood were an important function of heraldry in the 13th century, a fact borne witness to by the graffiti, such as this crest, left behind by crusading knights in the Church of the Nativity in Bethlehem.

▶ Three versions of the Brackenhaupt (hound's head) crest.
1 Crest of Lentold von Regensburg.
2 The differenced crest of Oettingen.
3 The crest later adopted by Hohenzollern of Brandenburg.

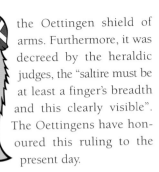

CREST PARTNERSHIP

On 10 April 1317 Burgrave Friedrich IV of Nuremberg, a member of the Hohenzollern family, purchased a new crest for his arms from Lentold von Regensburg. Burgrave Friedrich paid 36 marks for the privilege, an enormous sum in those days. The crest in question was a golden Brackenhaupt, a hound's head with red ears. At the same time, Lentold von Regensburg reserved the right of certain of his relations to use the same crest during their lifetime. In September of the same year, the Burgrave exacted from Lentold another document in which the latter confirmed that, "I give full power and right to the Burgrave to use the crest as if I were present myself, in case others should contest his right to use it."

Prior to the purchase, the Burgrave had entered into a *Helmgerossenschaft* (crest partnership) with the Counts of Oettingen, the crest in this case being a *Schirmbrett* (wooden panel) ornamented with peacock feathers, typical of German crests of the period. This crest partnership had existed between the two families principally because of a marriage alliance, but had lapsed by the time that the Burgrave purchased the second crest from Lentold von Regensburg. However, the Oettingens attempted to cling to their interest in a possible succession to the estates of the Burgrave and promptly adopted the *Brackenhaupt*, much to the annoyance of the Hohenzollerns.

A lengthy heraldic dispute now ensued, which was resolved in 1381 when a panel of noble and royal arbitrators decided that the Oettingens could continue to use the gold hound's head, but would have to difference its red ears with a white saltire from the Oettingen shield of arms. Furthermore, it was decreed by the heraldic judges, the "saltire must be at least a finger's breadth and this clearly visible". The Oettingens have honoured this ruling to the present day.

GIFTS OF FRIENDSHIP

On some occasions, German knights purchased the arms of others. In 1368 Hans Traganer, sold his arms and crest to Pilgrim von Wolfsthal, vowing that he and his offspring, would from that moment forever cease to use their arms.

Arms and crests were not only sold but also handed over as gifts. In 1286, Duke Otto of Austria bestowed upon Count William of Julich his crest – a crown with peacock feathers – as a mark of friendship. In 1350, at the Holy Sepulchre in Jerusalem, Matthew de Roya bestowed upon the knight Hartmann von Cronenberg, his crest of a boar's head. Heraldry was symbolically important in medieval society in many different ways.

▼ Alliances through marriage are recorded through a heraldic pedigree of the English family of Hesketh, 1594.

THE ARMS OF WOMEN

From the evidence of seals, it would seem that between the 13th and 15th centuries it became customary for European noblewomen to use the arms of their fathers and husbands on shields alone, without a crest. The seals themselves were often of an oval shape, similar to those of ecclesiastical institutions and clerics. As with the seals of armigerous men, those of armigerous women also often show the bearer herself, sometimes holding a shield in each hand. Some medieval monuments also show women bearing shields.

STATUS IN THE FAMILY

Although heraldry by its nature related to the individual, it quickly became the ideal medium to denote noble alliances, none more so than marriage. By the 15th century a complex system of marks and marrying of arms could show the viewer the exact status of the per-

▼ In the formative period of heraldry, 1150–1300, it is not uncommon to find women depicted with shields of their family arms, as on this Welsh lady's tomb in the Priory Church, Abergavenny.

son or persons whose arms they were studying. Sons, daughters, wives and widows were all able to denote their place in the family unit. Furthermore, the family could show its alliance with other families of noble status through the heraldic pedigree. In Britain, this was particularly true during the Tudor and Stuart periods, when the old nobility was increasingly on the defensive against merchants and other "newly made men" who were keen to acquire the trappings of gentility, including of course, family arms.

The clues to marital alliances, so important to the nobility of Europe, and the symbols of marital status and placing in the family unit, are complex and evolved over centuries. These are ongoing, with new rulings being enacted in recent years by the heraldic authorities of Canada and England on the rights of daughters and married women.

◄ The armorial garments of this medieval English lady were probably never worn but were simply an illustrative device to proclaim her noble status on funerary memorials and manuscripts.

▲ Joan, Countess of Surrey's seal, c1347, is perhaps the origin of the lozenge shape that was later chosen to display a woman's arms.

THE LOZENGE

A shield, being an article of warfare, was traditionally associated with men, and as such it was not considered appropriate for women. From the late medieval period, a diamond-shaped device – the lozenge – came into use for the armigerous lady

▼ Three generations of English women. From left: a widow with impaled arms, not an heiress; her daughter, a widow heiress; her granddaughter, a spinster, quartering her father and mother's arms.

▲ *A depiction of the arms of Queen Juliana of the Netherlands, before her succession to the throne, as Princess of Oranje-Nassau, Duchess of Mecklenburg.*

although, like so much in heraldry, just when the diamond was first used in this way is not clear. A remarkable English seal has survived from around 1347 for Joan, daughter of Henrie Count de Barre, widow of John de Warrenne, Earl of Surrey. Included in the seal's complex design are five tiny lozenges, the central lozenge bears the arms of Warenne, the lozenges in the flanks, of de Barre, and those above and below the arms of England – Countess Joan's mother was Eleanor, daughter of King Edward I of England. The seal is also diapered with castles and lions rampant for the countess's grandmother, Eleanor of Castile, first wife of King Henry.

By the 15th century the diamond or lozenge had become the normal platform for the display of the single woman's arms in Britain, France and the Low Countries, and so it continues to this day, the somewhat harsh shape being softened at times into the oval. However, whereas the oval has sometimes been used by men, the lozenge seems an entirely female device.

The unmarried woman simply uses her father's arms on the lozenge or oval, sometimes accompanied by a blue bow and ribbon, a symbol of maidenhood. (A heraldic writer in the 1800s suggested that unmarried spinsters in danger of remaining so should unite in an "order of the lozenge" and advertise for partners.)

While a bachelor is entitled to the family arms on a shield surmounted by helm, crest and motto, in most heraldic traditions a woman, married or not, cannot bear a crest. In Germany an unmarried daughter can bear the shield of her father's arms surmounted by a wreath or torse. In Scotland, a woman who is a clan chief is entitled to bear the crest above a lozenge or oval.

▼ *The lozenge is rather a hard shape and attempts were made to "feminize" it, as in this 18th-century display of the arms of the Duchess of Kendal, mistress of King George I of England.*

IMPALEMENT AND MARRIAGE

When marriage was depicted on seals and monuments in the early days of heraldry, it tended to be by way of complete shields of arms for the families of both the husband and the wife, shown separately. In the late 13th century a process started by which two separate arms were placed side by side on a shield. At first, in order to fit both arms on to a single shield, each was simply chopped in half, or "dimidiated", in a somewhat unfortunate way. This curious marriage of two separate arms did not persist for long, and by the end of the 14th century the practice of showing the full set of charges for both coats on one shield had become the norm. In heraldic terms, the wife is called "femme" and her husband "baron", which in this context does not indicate rank.

DIMIDIATION

An example of the earlier practice of dimidiation can be seen in the arms used by Margaret of France after her marriage in 1299 to Edward I of England. Before marriage, the Queen as a daughter of France would simply have borne the ancient arms of France. Queen Margaret's seal shows her shield divided in half vertically, with the lion of England for her husband on the dexter half, and the lilies of France on the sinister side. As both

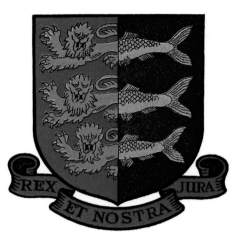

▲ Dimidiation threw up some curious creatures, such as in the arms of the English port of Great Yarmouth. Here the royal lions of England have their hind parts replaced with herrings' tails.

charges are cut in half by the dividing line, the front half of the English lion is married to the fleur de lis of France.

Not only marital coats suffered from dimidiation. The arms of some cities and towns (the English Cinq Ports being the most famous examples) also showed heraldic alliances in such a fashion, and dimidiation could result in some fascinating combinations. It is slightly modified in the arms of the Czech town of Zlonice.

▲ In much of Europe, when two arms are shown for husband and wife, the charges are turned to face each other; in heraldic terminology they are "respectant".

Here the sinister half of a black eagle is dimidiated with a coat per fess but, while most of the eagle is sliced through, its head is left intact and allowed to enter the dexter half of the shield.

IMPALEMENT

The word "impalement" sounds like some medieval form of torture (just as the "bend sinister" of the bastard seems to imply some hideous heraldic secret), but the term is simply used to denote a side-by-side alliance of two coats on a shield. It was the practice for which dimidiation paved the way, the difference being that impalement shows the charges of the two coats in their entirety. The only exception is made for some bordures or charges said to be "in orle", or following the edge of the shield. These are still cut off by the vertical division of the two coats. The placing of two or more separate coats of arms on a single shield is called "marshalling".

Marital impalement is particularly observed in British heraldry, yet even here there are differences in practice. In England it is used when the wife has brothers who will carry on her own family arms, so that she is not classed as a heraldic heiress. In such a case the children born to the marriage inherit only the arms of the father. In Scotland, however, impalement is used in

▲ The dimidiated arms of Margaret of France after her marriage to King Edward I of England in 1299.

◀ In the arms of the town of Zlonice in the Czech Republic, the eagle's head transcends the impalement line.

▲ *This hatchment for a Dutch widow has her arms upon an oval-shaped shield as opposed to a lozenge.*

▲ *The impaled arms of a French princess. The lozenge is within the cordelière.*

▼ *The arms of a Dutch widow impaled with those of her husband and surrounded by shields recording marital alliances.*

▲ *A page from a Flemish pedigree and armorial of 1590, with the husband's achievement (centre) turned towards his wife's lozenge.*

both cases, whether the wife is a heraldic heiress or not. In France and the Low Countries no distinction is made.

In much of Europe a marital coat is denoted not so much by impalement as by two separate shields set "accolee", or side by side. Often these are tilted to touch each other at one corner, and the charges of each shield are turned towards each other, instead of facing to the left as is the more normal position. Should a bend be included in the design of the husband's arms this too is turned, giving it the appearance of a bend sinister. In Germany the shields of both husband and wife are surmounted by helm and crest; a display of two complete achievements is there known as an *Allianzwappen* or *Ehewappen*.

WIVES AND WIDOWS

In a recent ruling, the English kings of arms ordained that a married woman may bear her paternal arms, even if her hus-band is not armigerous, on a shield or banner differenced by a small escutcheon of a contrasting tincture in the corner or elsewhere on the shield, in a manner most suitable to the design.

Furthermore, the ruling states that even if the wife comes from an armigerous family she may bear her husband's arms alone, the shield charged with a small lozenge. Widows revert to the lozenge but with the impaled arms of husband and wife. In Europe it has often been the practice for the widow's lozenge to be placed within a "cordelière" (knotted cord). In England a divorced woman may revert to a lozenge of her family's arms, her divorced status shown by the differencing of a small mascle in some suitable place on the lozenge.

HEIRESSES AND SIMPLE QUARTERING

From the late medieval period onwards, pedigrees and other family papers and memorials show the contents of shields being marshalled in an ever more complex way, through a heraldic stratagem known as "quartering". This was a method used throughout European heraldry, principally to display alliances made through marriage, and it indicates how estates or fiefdoms were established and built up through such alliances.

As with other aspects of heraldry, quartering differed in various minor ways between nations, and it is important to remember this when viewing a quartered shield. Mistakes can be made when reading the messages that are declared, unless the rules of the nation in which the arms evolved are also taken into account.

▼ Many a church interior shows the pomp and piety of the local nobility through memorials that are bright with heraldry. This English couple have their family arms above their heads while the husband's family, the Newdegates, celebrate a previous marriage with quartered shields at the head and base of the memorial.

ESCUTCHEON OF PRETENCE

In England, a heraldic quartering occurs after a marriage with a heraldic heiress – a woman who has no brothers, so that her family lacks a direct male heir. In such a case, the husband, instead of placing his wife's arms beside his on the marital shield (as an impalement), places them upon a small shield in the centre of his own arms. This small shield is called an "escutcheon of pretence", the husband in this case "pretending" to be the male head of his wife's family. Any children born to such a marriage are entitled to bear not only their father's arms, but also those of their mother (on a shield for a son, or a lozenge for a daughter), as quartering.

HOW QUARTERING WORKS

In the simplest case, where just one heraldic heiress has married into the family, the shield or lozenge is divided in four quarters. The patrimonial arms appear in the top left and bottom right hand quarters (numbered 1 and 4) and the arms of the heiress are placed in the top right and bottom left hand quarters (2 and 3).

The next heraldic heiress who marries into the family again takes her family arms to her husband, who places them in the centre of the already quartered arms, as another escutcheon of pretence. In the next generation, these arms appear as a new third quarter (bottom left) of the quartered arms. The shield should always have an equal number of quarterings (although this was not so in past times), and until a third heiress enters the scheme, the patrimonial arms are repeated in the fourth quarter

▲ In England the widow who is also a heraldic heiress reverts to the lozenge of her husband's arms with an escutcheon of pretence – here the arms of Nelson are shown with a quartered escutcheon.

(bottom right). This is all well and good until a fourth heiress is married.

Supposedly there can only be four quarters which have all now been used up, but heraldry can be pragmatic and the term "quarter" is used for any number of separate arms on one shield. It is possible for a newly armigerous man, without any quarterings to his family arms, to marry the heiress of an ancient family with many quarterings. The children of such a marriage will bear not only their father's arms, but also all the quarters of their mother's arms. Therefore in just two generations a shield can go from simple to complex.

NATIONAL VARIATIONS

Elsewhere, the adding of quarterings and the nature of what in England would be thought of as an escutcheon of pretence, have their own system and meaning. In Scotland the escutcheon is reserved for an important fiefdom, usually one associated with a title held by the holder of a peerage, while in Germany the escutcheon is normally reserved for the family arms and the quarterings are kept for the arms associated with various fiefdoms and families that brought territory to the estate now held by the family.

In Britain more than one crest can be borne by a family, usually when two or more surnames are used in a hyphenated form. Noble German families usually place a crested helm above the shield for each quartering, and some families of courtly or princely rank may display as many as 20 crests above the shield. In Scandinavia as

▼ *The escutcheon of pretence for an heiress is clearly displayed in the centre of her husband's shield.*

a family was advanced to a higher degree the arms tended to be augmented with the addition of quarterings – the escutcheon being kept for the original family arms.

In England and Wales, marriage to a non-armigerous wife was simply indicated by a blank impalement or escutcheon. It seems an absurdity, but some authorities thought it necessary to show the exact heraldic status of the husband. The pedigree books of the House of Lords for peers of the realm record many such heraldic curiosities. No similar practices seem to be employed outside England and Wales.

◄ *The arms of the Counts von Creutz in the House of Nobility, Helsinki. The background quarters were added as the family passed up the ranks of the nobility.*

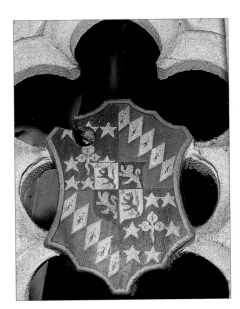

▲ *In Germany and Austria the escutcheon is usually reserved for the original arms.*

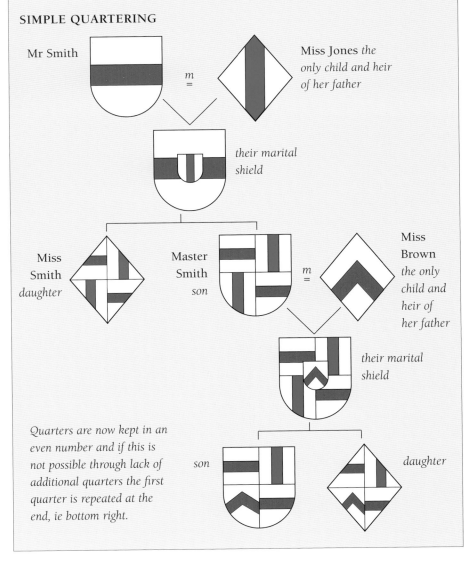

SIMPLE QUARTERING

Mr Smith — *m* — Miss Jones *the only child and heir of her father*

their marital shield

Miss Smith *daughter* — Master Smith *son* — *m* — Miss Brown *the only child and heir of her father*

their marital shield

son — *daughter*

Quarters are now kept in an even number and if this is not possible through lack of additional quarters the first quarter is repeated at the end, ie bottom right.

COMPLEX QUARTERINGS

In Britain, families of ancient lineage may have shields bearing many heraldic quarterings, sometimes running into hundreds. Heraldists divide into two schools of thought about multiple quarterings. There are those who despise such a shield, believing it to be a vulgar show of pretension. Others see it as a welcome chance for a piece of heraldic detective work – working back through the various quarterings with the help of pedigrees. A many-quartered shield can lead the viewer into all kinds of adventures when trying to decipher it: they may make their own family connection, or turn up stories of murder, mayhem, heroes and heroines. It can be fun to make a map locating all the families illustrated on just one shield, though in some cases the map will have to be very large.

REPEATED QUARTERS

Should an heiress whose family has amassed its own heraldic quarterings marry into the family, these are in turn placed in their own chronological order. The English scheme provides the viewer with no clue as to which heiress brought in which quarters, but Scottish heraldry provides the clue by keeping such a set of quarters together in an impartable group or "grand quarter".

In Britain, should an armiger have no sons but several daughters, each is classed as a co-heiress, and all are equally entitled to transmit their father's arms to any children they may have in marriage. Looking closely at the grand quarterings of the Dukes of Buckingham and Chandos, it is possible to see that some individual quarters are actually identical with others dotted around the shield, because they represent marriages to the descendants of co-heiresses, and since at any time the English aristocracy represents less than one per cent of the nation's population, marriage within that group is bound to throw up such heraldic curiosities.

The great Anglo-Norman family of de Clare terminated with the three daughters and co-heiresses of Gilbert de Clare, Earl

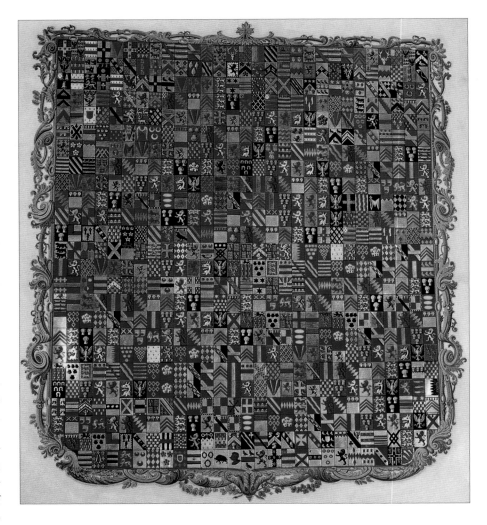

of Hereford and Gloucester (their brother, Gilbert, having been killed in 1313). These grand ladies were able to transmit the arms of de Clare, Or three chevronels Gules, to their children, who also married into great families. It was therefore possible for a family such as the Grenvilles to marry into other families of rank and antiquity, each of whom represented an heiress of the de Clares.

PEDIGREES

In continental Europe it was at certain times necessary for noble families to prove their ancestry by showing descent from 16 great-great-grandparents, all of whom were expected to be armigerous. Such an armorial pedigree is called "Proof of Seize-quartiers". Not only was such a proof desirable for those wishing to attend a

▲ *Possibly the most impressive collection of quartering ever used for an English family, these are the 719 quarters of the Dukes of Buckingham and Chandos.*

royal court or trying to enter one of the various orders of chivalry, but also for those attempting to become officers in certain military regiments.

A lesser pedigree was also often used in continental Europe for memorials, gravestones and the like. In such cases, the shield of the deceased would be placed in the centre of the memorial, and down either side would be shown all the shields of arms of the parents, grandparents and sometimes great-grandparents, both on the male and female side. These heraldic pedigrees in stone can still be seen in many European churches.

COMPLEX QUARTERING

This chart gives an example of how quarters accumulate over the generations, as heiresses marry into the family, and yet more quarters are added to the shield.

Mr A *has no sons, his 2 daughters are termed co-heiresses and can equally impart their family arms to their children as a quartering.*

Mr B   Miss Sarah A
m
=

Miss Jane A   Mr F
m
=

Mr C   *The marital shield*

The marital shield

An only daughter Miss C   *m* =   *A son* Mr B (2nd)

Miss F

Mr D   *The marital shield*

An only daughter Miss D   Mr B (3rd)
m =   Miss B   Mr E (1st)
m =

The marital shield   *The marital shield*

Mr B (4th)   Mr E (2nd)   *Miss B is not an heiress as she has a brother. Her children — Mr E 2nd and Miss E inherit only the arms of their father*

DIFFERENCE MARKS AND CADENCY

It is said that the *raison d'être* of heraldry is its ability to celebrate the individual's identity in visual terms, so that the coat of arms can be thought of as the pictorial signature of the bearer. Just how individual the arms are, in fact, depends on the nationality of the user. For instance, in Poland an identical coat of arms may be borne by many different families with no blood relationship because it is used by a whole tribe, or *ród*. In some countries, personal shields are distinguished only between branches of royal houses. In Scotland families update their heraldry through a process of rematriculating their arms through the court of Lord Lyon. The distinguishing features used for this are known as "cadency" or "difference marks".

▼ *English cadency marks, as set out in the 6th edition of John Guillim's* A Display of Heraldry *(1724).*

SONS AND DAUGHTERS

Much of heraldry can be accused of sexism, as daughters are not considered as important as their brothers. In England, until recently, they were afforded little notice at all unless they were classed as heraldic heiresses. Even then, should there be several daughters and no sons, the daughters had no marks of difference or cadency between them, each bearing an identical lozenge of their father's arms. On the Iberian peninsula the situation seems to be much more sensible, and the female side of a family is considered every bit as important as that of the male. In Portugal anyone is entitled to choose their surname and arms from whichever side of the family they wish, and a system of difference marks denotes from which side of the family the arms are derived and whether they come from parents or grandparents.

CANADIAN CADENCY MARKS

These are the new marks of cadency given by Canada to each daughter of an armigerous family.

First, second and third daughters.

Fourth, fifth and sixth daughters.

Seventh, eighth and ninth daughters.

The newest national heraldic authority, that of Canada, has also given difference marks to each daughter in the same way that sons have their coats differenced.

MARKS OF CADENCY

While difference marks may be applied to a variety of family and heraldic relationships, cadency tends to be used to indicate sons. It is very much the preserve of English heraldry, in which a set of small marks are placed upon the shield for male children up to the ninth son. The heraldic writer Beryl Platt sees their origin in the symbols adopted by the heirs of Charlemagne. She believes that the Count of Boulogne, whose family used these marks, had set great store by the dialogues of the Emperor Charlemagne with his confessor Alcuin, and would have found references there to heavenly and natural symbols as inspirational devices. In Boulogne the sun stood for the Count, the crescent for his second son, the star for his third son, and the bird for his fourth son. The cadency marks of later children could also have been taken from Charlemagne's

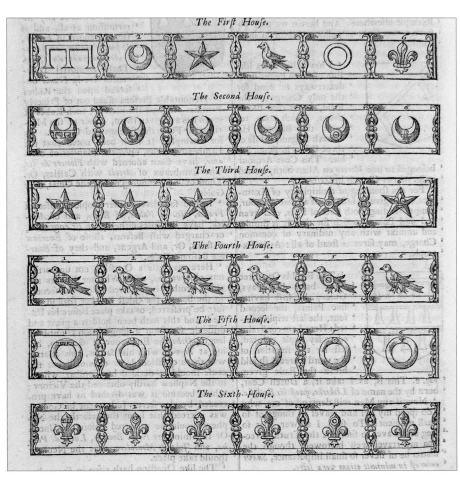

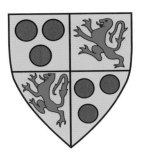 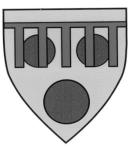 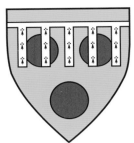 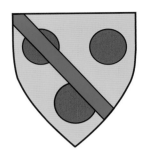 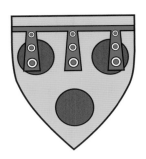

▲ *Medieval difference marks for members of the Courteney family of Devon, England.*

dialogues. The most important and frequently used mark is the "label". It is an addition to arms not only in English heraldry, but also in Scotland, France, Spain, Portugal, Belgium and Italy. In England it has long been used as the mark of the eldest son, and a plain white label is given to the heir apparent of the sovereign.

The origin of the label might be found in the sculpted shield of a 13th-century English knight, probably Sir Alexander Giffard, in Boyton, Wiltshire. The shield bears the ancient arms of Giffard – Gules three lions passant Argent. Over the whole shield there is the label, most probably representing a cord stretched over the charges on the shield. From the cord were attached several ribbons, and at this early stage their number seems not to have been of any significance (Sir Alexander's shield shows five

ribbons). By the late 15th century, however, three ribbons or "points" seem to have been fixed as the number for an eldest son. Such is the finesse of the stone carvers' work at Boyton, the contrasting crudeness of the label shows clearly its deliberately temporary nature. It would seem that the eldest son was expected to remove the label when he became head of the house.

Other sons, from the second to the ninth, all have their own cadency marks, but there is no rule about the use of such marks (which are usually placed in the centre chief point). It is possible for sons of sons of sons to place their own cadency mark on a cadency mark, and so on, but this may become an absurdity as the mark becomes so small as to be useless. Furthermore, should any quarterings be added by a family branch (through marriage to a heraldic heiress) this would in itself be considered sufficient difference as to negate any need for a cadency mark.

Adopted children may use the arms of their adoptive parents (after a royal licence has been granted to do so), charged with two interlaced links of a chain. In certain cases, an English family may assume the arms of another through royal licence, usually because of a so-called "name and arms clause" in the will of the last of a line. Often this was done when the father of an heiress wished to see his family arms and name continue, as on the shield of Vere Fane-Bennett Stanford of Preston, England. His wife's arms appear twice, once on an escutcheon and also as the first quarter of the main shield, differenced by a cross crosslet, as there was no descent by blood.

Recently English married women have been allowed to bear (if they should wish to) their own family arms alone on a shield, as opposed to their marital arms. This is made clear by the inclusion of a small blank escutcheon on the main shield, as seen on the arms of Margaret Thatcher.

▼ *The shield of Sir Alexander Giffard of Boyton shows how the first labels might have been temporarily constructed.*

▼ *A blank escutcheon in the arms of Baroness Thatcher denotes that these are her own arms, rather than her husband's.*

▼ *The arms of Vere Fane-Bennett Stanford, who assumed the arms of his wife's family, differenced by cross crosslet.*

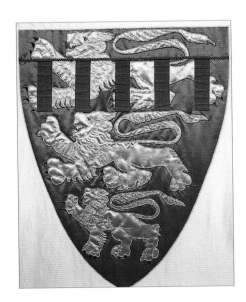

ILLEGITIMACY

We have seen how certain marks have become associated with children born to armigerous parents, albeit those quite obviously married. What, then, is the position of those children born out of wedlock – the illegitimate? The matter is ambiguous at best. Nowadays, in many countries, the illegitimate child is entitled to most, if not all, of the legal rights of a legitimate child, but in previous ages he or she was considered to be without parentage, without name and unable to inherit titles and estates. Although on these terms such children may seem not to have occupied a very enviable position, in truth, in many noble houses, more affection was given to them by their father than his legitimate issue, who, having an automatic right to succession, might be more prepared to rebel against parental control.

THE BATON AND BEND SINISTER

In 1463 the chief herald of the Duke of Burgundy wrote, "a bastard may carry the arms of his father with a baton sinister", thereby making mention of just one of the many heraldic marks used to differ the arms of the illegitimate over the centuries. No hard and fast rule existed in most nations as to what marks the illegitimate should bear, so long as they were sufficiently distinct from the normal cadency

▲ Even the heraldic badge could be used to show illegitimacy. Here the Beaufort portcullis is so differenced for Sir Charles Somerset KG.

▲ The arms of John Beaufort, son of John of Gaunt, before his legitimization; confusingly the bend is in the normal position.

marks of legitimate sons. The bend sinister was a popular mark to denote illegitimacy. By the 17th century this had often shrunk to a baton sinister. (The modern meaning of the word "sinister" has given such a mark an unfortunate reputation, whereas of course, it really refers only to the direction of the bend – top right to bottom left from the bearer's point of view.)

In England the baton sinister became associated with royal bastards, who were often given such a mark charged in some personal way. One illegitimate son of William IV (1830–7), the "Sailor King", had his baton sinister charged with golden anchors, while others might have their batons charged with a royal badge such as the white rose.

THE BORDURE

In 1397 the children born to John of Gaunt and his mistress, Katherine Swynford (whom he married in that year) were declared legitimate by an act unique in English history. Soon afterwards the children, the Beauforts, were permitted to bear the quartered arms of France and England within a bordure compony (a border divided into segments) of John of Gaunt's own livery, white and blue.

Curiously, the bordure compony placed around the arms of the Beauforts after their legitimization came to be used as a mark to denote bastardy, the baton sinister being used more often for royal illegitimates. In Scottish heraldry, the bordure compony is the only recognized mark of illegitimacy. Members of the Stewart family, however, bore arms differenced not only by two bordures compony, but by a bendlet sinister compony as well. Something of a milestone was reached in 1780 when the heralds granted the arms (as a quartering) of the arms of Sacheverell within a bordure wavy to a descendant, John Zachary, the

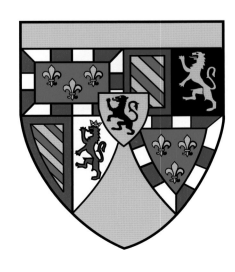

▲ ▼ Two 15th-century examples of arms for two illegitimate sons of the dukes of Burgundy. Their fathers' quarters are shown on voided shields.

▲ *In an unusual combination, the bordure added to the Beaufort arms after their legitimization and the bend sinister of illegitimacy appear on the one shield for Sir Charles Somerset KG (d1526), natural son of Henry Beaufort, third Duke of Somerset.*

bordure wavy in this case being used to denote illegitimate descent. From that time onward the bordure wavy has been mainly used for the English illegitimate offspring, and their descendants.

In Scotland the crest is not differenced but in England it is, and illegitimate descent can be denoted either by pallets wavy, saltires wavy or bendlets sinister.

▼ ► *These arms were granted in 1806 to Maria and William Legh, two of the seven illegitimate children of Colonel Thomas Legh, of Lyme.*

HERALDIC INHERITANCE

In England it is necessary for the father to acknowledge paternity if the illegitimate child wishes to claim heraldic descent. A royal licence can then be issued granting use of the father's arms, duly differenced by certain marks (usually the bordure wavy) denoting illegitimacy. But the process is lengthy and requires the sovereign's authorization. The heralds may therefore suggest that instead of this traditional procedure the illegitimate child petitions for new arms that are based on the arms of the father.

It is generally held that illegitimate children cannot inherit any quarterings that were previously built up by their father's family, yet there is much evidence to show that they often have. A further curiosity in English heraldry is that a female bastard is treated as the heraldic heiress and can transmit her father's arms, with a suitable mark of difference, to her children. As for modern and more enlightened times we may look to the heraldry of the Republic of Ireland, where illegitimacy has no place.

◄ *The arms of Sir Richard de Clarendon, illegitimate son of Edward the Prince of Wales, utilize the feathers from his father's shield for peace.*

▲ *In the Sacheverell arms granted to John Zachary, 1780, a bordure wavy was used to denote illegitimacy for the first time.*

HOW A MEDIEVAL FAMILY USED ITS ARMS

Si monumentum requiris, circumspice ("If you would see his monument, look around"): these words, carved above the north door of St Paul's Cathedral in the City of London, refer to the cathedral's designer, Sir Christopher Wren. Yet the very same words could have been used by many men centuries before Sir Christopher's age, who, through heraldry on castle and in church, sought to ensure their family's and their own immortality.

One medieval family of the West of England, the Hungerfords of Farleigh Castle, afford an example of the none too subtle way in which the nobility of Europe sought to stamp its authority over vast tracts of land and all that lived upon it. In stone, stained glass, parchment and needlepoint, the Hungerfords and many of their kind used heraldry to make a statement: "I am my arms. Hurt them and you hurt me – at your great peril be it."

▼ *On the ruins of Farleigh Hungerford Castle, the family arms above the main gate still proclaim the Hungerfords' lordship.*

ASSERTION OF IDENTITY

The Hungerfords were not remarkable in any way, but were typical of their times: sometimes cultured, sometimes violent, self-made, monied, landed, immensely proud, medieval in thought and deed. The family enjoyed its heyday in the late 14th and early 15th centuries, just at the time when the rival royal houses of York and Lancaster were flexing their muscles. It also happened to be the peak of that English heraldic phenomenon, the badge or cognizance; and the Hungerfords made the fullest possible use of their own device – a sickle or, its variation, three interlaced sickles – in many different ways.

Heraldry played a large part in the noble family's daily life. The Hungerfords stamped their arms on seals, barns, outbuildings and chantries, and set their sickles on seats, ceilings and church towers. Walter, 1st Baron Hungerford, a friend and adviser to the Lancastrian kings, had his arms set, as was his right as a Knight of the Garter, within the Chapel of St George in Windsor Castle itself. At court

▲ *A roof boss in St Thomas's Church in Salisbury denoting the trappings of patronage. It was the Hungerford family's large donations that helped to pay for the church's restoration in the early 1600s.*

he would probably have donned his great collar of "Ss", the livery collar of the dynasty he served so faithfully.

THE ACQUISITION OF ARMS

Although not perhaps remarkable in their class and time, the Hungerfords are intriguing in their use of arms, possibly taking as their own the arms of the Heytesbury family (Per pale indented Gules and Vert a chevron Or), whose

▼ *The quartered arms of Heytesbury and FitzJohn (Hungerford) appear in an elaborate medieval tiled floor from their former property at Heytesbury.*

▲ *The much-used sheaf and sickle crest of the Hungerfords is carved in stone on the roof of St Thomas's Church, Salisbury.*

▼ *The Hungerfords made full use of heraldic seals. The top seal, of Sir Robert Hungerford before 1449, differences not only the arms but the banners, crest and badge of his father, Lord Walter, while the bottom one also includes the supporters.*

heiress had married a Hungerford. They also seem to have done the same with the arms of another family, FitzJohn of Cherhill (Sable two bars Argent in chief three plates), which later became the acknowledged arms of Hungerford.

The Hungerford crest of a "garb" (a wheatsheaf) between two sickles may also have been adopted from that of another family, Peverell; such arms of alliance were not unusual at the time. The Hungerfords had most probably originated as lower gentry and were non-armigerous, becoming so through marriage with the heiresses of more well-to-do families. Even the nature of the garb in the Hungerford arms has an element of mystery about it – is it in fact a sheaf of wheat or pepper, a play on the name Peverell? The Hungerfords delighted in the use of their sickles, often charging their memorials and property with interlacings of sickle, a design well suited to many household ornaments and items of furniture.

In the will of Lord Walter Hungerford, Knight of the Garter (proved at Croydon, 21 August 1447), his son Robert was left

▲ *Along with other families of their time, the Hungerfords took the arms of more influential families for their own. In time the bars and roundels of the FitzJohns became the accepted arms of Hungerford. They also changed their crest from the talbot's head to the garb of the Peverells.*

"2 altar cloths of red crimson velvet, with diverse compresses de sykeles curiously embroidered…my great alms dish of silver having on each side a lion supporting my coat of arms; and a pair of silver dishes bearing knots of sickles". Sir Robert Hungerford was, according to his father's will, to bequeath these items to his heir.

The Hungerfords, proud and privileged as they undoubtedly were, lived in a troubled age. In the records of the time we can read of a rising in 1400 against King Henry IV, during which the rebels took several of the King's "lieges" (lords) prisoner. They compelled Lord Walter, "the King's Knight, to go with them and robbed him of the King's Livery called 'Colere' [the collar of Ss] which he was wearing, worth £20", an enormous sum in those distant days.

▲ *Like his father, Robert, 2nd Baron Hungerford was a staunch supporter of the House of Lancaster, and proudly wore the collar of Ss of that house.*

Times were to get better for Lord Walter, for in December 1418 he was rewarded with the Lordship of Homet in Normandy in return for an annual fee of a lance to which was attached a fox's brush (tail), one of the heraldic badges of Henry IV. However, a large part of the Hungerford revenues which arose from the acquisition of spoils in the French wars were used to bail out Lord Walter's grandson, Sir Robert, who was taken prisoner at the Battle of Castillon in 1453, a battle which brought the Hundred Years' War to a close with defeat for the English. One of the members of the deputation sent over to France to treat with Sir Robert's captors was Chester Herald – fulfilling one of the many duties undertaken by the heralds of the time.

HERALDRY AND ETERNITY

The Hundred Years' War, the Black Death and death in childbirth were among many perils the Hungerfords had to face, just as they reached the peak of their power in the English West Country. Beyond death, there was Purgatory, that period in which souls were lodged in Heaven's waiting room, waiting for their family to purchase a promotion heavenwards through prayer and good deeds. Here too, heraldry had its part to play. The Hungerfords, in common with many of their peers, endowed "chantries", chapels where the priests were employed solely to sing or chant daily masses for the noble benefactors. The wills of the latter make frequent mention of the trappings of their chantries and the priests that served

them. Presumably it was hoped that, if God in his Kingdom was looking down, he would notice the arms and badges of the noble family concerned and be grateful for the display. That, at any rate, must have been the thinking of Lord Walter, when he gave to the Abbey Church of Bath a cope of red velvet patterned with waves, and two other copes of gold damask velvet, that was "worked with myne armes for better memory".

The theme was taken up in the will of Lord Walter's daughter-in-law, the formidable Margaret Botreaux, Lady Hungerford. In the document she bequeaths to the Priory of Launceston (in Cornwall) a pair of vestments of red and green (the Hungerford livery colours) with the arms of Hungerford and Botreaux on the cross, and a further new pair of vestments to be worked with the arms of Hungerford, Beaumont and Botreaux. At

▼ *The finesse of the medieval craftsman is apparent in this complex seal design of Margaret Botreaux, widow of Robert, 2nd Baron Hungerford.*

▲ *Heraldry could be used in the most mundane ways. Here it embellishes the lock plate of the family vault at Farleigh Hungerford.*

▲ *Ever self-publicists, members of the Hungerford family placed their heraldry on all kinds of property. This interlaced sickle badge was uncovered recently above a false ceiling in a farmhouse, some five centuries after its crude manufacture.*

▼ *Keeping the money in the family, a Hungerford marries his cousin: the crescent, centre left, denotes the younger branch on these impaled arms.*

Salisbury Cathedral, the wonderful altar cloths that the Lady Margaret gave included several bearing Lord Hungerford's crest and arms. Even the chantry chapels themselves, as in the case of the Hungerford Chapel in Wellow church, near Bath, might be brightly painted in the family livery colours.

On Salisbury Plain, over the borders of Wiltshire into Somerset and Gloucester and far and wide in the West Country, the Hungerford name spread itself. Whenever they acquired land, and wherever they had their souls prayed for, they stamped their authority through heraldry. Even on their last journey, entombed in their coffins, the Hungerfords could still afford a final nod to their arms, as the lock panel on their own family vault at Farleigh Castle was charged with the Hungerford shield. So famous were they in the West Country that other noble families in the area were keen to show an attachment to them through arms. In the 18th century, long after the Hungerfords had left the Plain, the Pleydell-Bouveries chose to use Lord Walter's chantry chapel in Salisbury Cathedral for their own pew, decorating it with over 50 shields of arms recording the Hungerford marriages and their descent from that family.

▲ *The priest of the Hungerford family at Wellow church, Somerset, was surrounded by the heraldry of those he was expected to pray for, from the family arms to their red and gold liveries used as ceiling patterns.*

▼ *In common with others in the exalted band of the Knights of the Garter, Walter, 1st Lord Hungerford's arms appear on his stall plate in St George's Chapel, Windsor.*

GLOSSARY

abatement: heraldic mark of dishonour

accolée: descriptive term for two coats of arms set side by side, to indicate marriage, with the charges on each facing each other

achievement: the complete display of armorial bearings

addorsed: of beasts, back to back

affronty: of a *charge*, facing the viewer

ailettes: "little wings", shoulder plates bearing the arms of the wearer

alwyte: bright steel armour from the late medieval period

Argent: silver

armed: of a human being, clothed in armour; of a beast, having teeth, beak or claws in a separate colour

armiger: a person who is entitled to bear arms

arming cap: a padded cap worn under a helmet

arming doublet: a long-sleeved, hip-length tunic worn as an undergarment for armour

armorial bearings: the symbols borne by an *armiger* to distinguish him or her from others

armorial: a roll or book listing *armorial bearings* arranged alphabetically by the names of the bearers

armory: the study of *coats of arms*, heraldry

at gaze: of deer, looking towards the viewer

attainder: the extinction of civil rights, including the right to bear arms or titles, following conviction for treason or felony

attitude: of a beast or human being, posture

attribute: of a beast or human being, a characteristic with which it is represented

attributed arms: arms devised posthumously for individuals who lived before the age of heraldry

augmentation: an addition to the arms that reflects the gratitude of the donor (usually a sovereign)

aventail: a chain mail neck guard

Azure: blue

bachelor: a knight of the lower order

badge: a heraldic device belonging to an *armiger*, worn by retainers

banner: a square or oblong flag bearing a knight's arms

bar: a narrow horizontal stripe

baron: heraldic term for a husband; also the lowest rank of the peerage

bascinet: a lightweight, close-fitting domed helmet

Bath, Order of the: a British chivalric order

baton: a narrow diagonal band which does not reach the edges of the shield

bedesman: or beadsman, someone who was employed to pray for another person or group of people

bend: a diagonal stripe on a shield, from *dexter* chief to *sinister* base

bend sinister: a diagonal stripe on a shield, from *sinister* chief to *dexter* base, often used as a mark of illegitimacy

bendlet: a narrow *bend*

bezant: a gold *roundel*

billet: a small rectangular *charge*

billetty: covered all over with *billets*

blazon: the verbal description of *armorial bearings*

Bleu celeste: sky blue

bonacon: a mythical heraldic beast

bordure: a narrow band around the edge of the shield

boss: a circular protruding central knob on a shield

brizure: a difference mark used in *cadency*

cadency: a system of small alterations and additions to differentiate the arms of children in a family from those of its head

canting: of arms, with a design that alludes to the name of the bearer, also known as punning arms

canton: a square section, smaller than a *quarter*, in the top *dexter* or *sinister* corner of a shield

chamfron: a horse's head-guard

chapeau: a hat with a turned-up fur lining, symbolizing dignity

charge: a device on a shield or other item

chequey: covered all over with squares of equal size, in two alternating colours

chevron: an inverted V-shaped stripe on a shield

chevronel: a small *chevron*, or bent *bar*, on a shield

chief: the upper third of the shield

cinquefoil: a stylized flower with five petals

cipher: a monogram

coat armour: a quilted linen garment worn over armour and emblazoned with *armorial bearings*

coat of arms: the common term for the heraldic shield

cockatrice: a mythical heraldic monster, part serpent and part cockerel

cognizance: a distinguishing *badge*

compartment: the representation of the ground or other surface on which the *supporters*, shield and motto stand

coronel: blunted, crown-shaped lance tip used in jousting

couchant: of a beast, lying down with head erect

counterchanged: descriptive of a partitioned shield where the disposition of *tinctures* on one side of the partition line is reversed on the other side

counterermine: see *ermines*

couped: of a *charge*, such as an arm or branch, clean cut

couter: armour worn to protect the elbow

crest: a three-dimensional object adorning the top of the helmet

cross crosslet: a cross with the end of each limb itself crossed

cuir-bouilli: leather boiled in oil to make it malleable

cuirass: plate armour for the torso

cuisse: leg armour

cushion: a *charge* in the shape of a cushion with tassels at the corners

dancetty: "dancing", of a *line of partition*, a zigzag with large indentations

degradation: demotion from knighthood

delf: a square geometric *charge*

dexter: right (from the point of view of the shield bearer)

diaper: an all-over pattern resembling designs woven into damask fabric

difference mark: a *charge* added to a shield to differentiate a branch of a family

dimidiated: an early form of *marshalling* arms by halving them

dovetailed: of a *line of partition*, like a joint in carpentry

embattled: of a *line of partition*, like battlements

engrailed: of a *line of partition*, scalloped, with the points facing outwards

ensign: to place a crown, coronet, cap, helmet or cross above, and touching, a *charge*

erased: of a *charge* such as a limb, torn off

ermine: one of the *furs*, white with black tails (the stoat's winter coat)

ermines or counterermine: one of the *furs*, black with white tails

erminites: like *ermine*, with a red spot on each side of the black tail

erminois: one of the *furs*, gold with black tails

escarbuncle: a wheel-like device with spokes radiating from the centre of the shield

escutcheon: a small shield

escutcheon of pretence: a small shield bearing the wife's family arms set in the centre of her husband's shield

estoile: star with wavy points

femme: heraldic term for a wife

fess: a horizontal stripe across the middle of the shield

field: the background *tincture* of the shield

fimbriated: of a *charge*, edged with a narrow band of another *tincture*

fitched: usually of a cross, pointed at the foot

flanches or flaunches: a pair of curved segments on each side of the shield

fleur de lis: a stylized heraldic lily

formy: of a cross, having triangular limbs wide at the ends and narrow at the centre

fountain: a *roundel* bearing blue and white wavy bars

fraise: a white *cinquefoil* representing the strawberry flower

fret: a *voided lozenge* interlaced with a *bendlet* and a *bendlet sinister*

fretty: covered all over with a grid of diagonal lines

fur: a *tincture* representing an animal pelt

fusil: an elongated *lozenge*

gambeson: a quilted undergarment worn with chain mail

gambs: animals' paws

garb: a sheaf (usually of wheat)

Garter King of Arms: the most senior English herald

Garter, Order of the: the senior order of knighthood in England

golpe: a purple *roundel*

gonfalone: a large flag often hung from a cross-beam

gonfalonier: a standard-bearer of the Church

gore: a portion of the shield cut off by a curved line, like a *flanch*, but ending in a point

gouttes: small *roundels* or droplets

goutty: covered all over with *gouttes*

great helm: a helmet made with a

series of hammered plates rising to a gradual point

greaves: leg-guards

griffin or gryphon: a mythical monster with the forepart of an eagle and the hindquarters of a lion

guardant: of a beast or human being, looking out of the shield at the viewer

guidon: a long flag used in battle as a marker or standard

guige: a strap to hold a shield when not in use

Gules: red

gusset: a side portion of the shield, cut off at top and bottom by diagonal lines

gyron: a wedge-shaped *charge*

gyronny: covered with *gyrons*, arranged around the centre of the shield

harness: a suit of armour

hatchment: a diamond-shaped board painted with a *coat of arms* to indicate the death of the bearer

heater shield: shield shaped like the base of a flatiron

heraldic heiress: the daughter of an *armiger*, who inherits his arms in the absence of any sons

hoist: the area at the top of a flag near the pole

honour point: the upper middle point of a shield

hurt: a blue *roundel*

imbrued: bloodied

impalement: the placing of two *coats of arms* side by side on a single shield

impress or impresa: a personal *badge* incorporating a motto

in chase: of deer, running

indented: of a *line of partition*, with small saw-like points

inescutcheon: a small shield borne in the centre of another shield

invected: as *engrailed*, with points facing inwards

jupon: a short, close-fitting quilted coat, usually decorated with the bearer's arms

king of arms: a senior herald

knight banneret: 1 a high-ranking knight in command of a body of

men; 2 a square or oblong banner denoting his presence in battle

label: a difference mark across the *chief* of the shield applied to the arms of a son, usually the heir

langued: of a beast, with a tongue in a separate colour

line of partition: a line delineating a division of the shield

lists: a jousting enclosure at a tournament

livery: the uniform worn by a lord's retainers, made in his colours

livery collar: a chain of office indicating allegiance

lodged: of a deer, lying down

lozenge: 1 a diamond-shaped *charge*; 2 a diamond-shaped device used to display the arms of women

Lyon, Lord: the chief herald in Scotland

mantling: material protecting the back and sides of the helmet and the wearer's neck

marshal: to combine two or more coats of arms on one shield

mascle: a *lozenge* with its centre removed

matriculation of arms: the updating of family arms in Scotland

maunch: a medieval sleeve with a hanging pocket

melée: a battle staged as a tournament event

mullet: a five-pointed star

mural coronet: a circlet of stone with battlements or columns

Murrey: mulberry, a purplish-red

nebuly: of a *line of partition*, shaped like the edges of clouds

nombril or navel point: the lower middle point of a shield

officer of arms: a herald

ogress: a black *roundel*

Or: gold

ordinary: 1 a basic geometric *charge* on a shield; 2 a *roll of arms* in which *coats of arms* are catalogued according to the charges they bear

orle: a narrow band following, but set in from, the edge of the shield

pageant helmet: a helmet with ornamental bars across the face

pairle: a division of the *field* into three sections radiating from the centre

pale: a vertical band down the middle of the shield

pall: a Y-shaped band on a shield

panache: a feathered *crest*

paper heraldry: a derogatory description of accessories, such as *crests*, designed after heraldry ceased to have a practical function, which could not have been used for their ostensible purpose

partition lines: see *lines of partition*

passant: of a beast, walking across the shield

patty: of a cross, having triangular limbs which are wide at the ends and narrow at the centre

pean: one of the *furs*, black with gold tails

pellet: a black *roundel*

pencil: a small *pennon*

pennon: a personal flag, long and tapering, with a rounded or divided end

peytrel: a horse's chest-plate

pheon: an arrowhead

pile: an *ordinary* consisting of a triangular wedge with one side along the top of the shield

plate: a silver *roundel*

point: the base of the shield cut off by a horizontal line

point champain: the base of the shield cut off by a shallow concave line

pomme: a green *roundel*

potent: in the shape of a crutch

proper: shown in natural colours or form

punning arms: see *canting*

Purpure: purple

pursuivant: a junior herald

quarter: 1 a *sub-ordinary* occupying the top *dexter* quarter of the shield; 2 to divide a shield into any number of divisions each bearing a different *coat of arms*

quatrefoil: a stylized four-petalled flower, similar to a clover leaf

queue fourchy: a forked tail

raguly: of a *line of partition*, like battlements but set obliquely

rampant: of a beast, rearing up to fight

recursant: usually of an eagle, displayed with its back towards the viewer

reguardant: looking backwards

respectant: of two beasts or human beings, looking at each other

reversed: upside-down

roll of arms: a herald's catalogue of *coats of arms*

roundel: a circular *charge*

rustre: a *charge* like a *lozenge* with a hole in the middle

Sable: black

saltire: a diagonal cross on a shield

Sanguine: blood red

segreant: of a *griffin*, rearing up to fight

sejant: of a beast, sitting upright facing *dexter*

semy: covered all over with small *charges*

sinister: left (from the point of view of the bearer of the shield)

springing: of a deer, leaping

stain: a heraldic colour that is not one of the primaries

standard: a long tapering flag in *livery* colours bearing the national emblem, usually placed at the commander's tent

statant: of a beast, standing facing *dexter*

sub-ordinary: one of the smaller, less frequently used geometric *charges*

supporters: figures supporting the shield of arms

surcoat: a quilted linen garment worn over armour and emblazoned with *coats of arms*

tabard: a short tunic emblazoned with *coats of arms* and worn by heralds

talbot: a large hunting hound, now extinct

targe: a shield

Tenny: tawny orange

Thistle, Order of the: the senior order of knighthood in Scotland

tierced in pairle: of a shield, divided in three in the form of a Y

tilt: a wooden jousting barrier

tincture: the generic term for heraldic colours, stains, metals and furs

torse: see *wreath*

tourney shield: a small rectangular shield, with a notch for a lance

tourteau: a red *roundel*

trapper: a development of the saddle-cloth which covered the horse entirely, decorated with *armorial bearings*

tressure: a narrow band following, but set in from, the edge of the shield, narrower than the *orle* but often doubled

tricking: a method of noting a *blazon* in shorthand

trippant: of deer, walking or trotting across a shield

vair: one of the *furs*, represented as a pattern of blue and white

Vert: green

visor: the opening front of a helmet

voided: of a *charge*, represented in outline only

vulned: of a beast, wounded and bleeding

wreath, torse: a twisted cord of material around the top of the helmet, below the crest

wyvern: a heraldic winged dragon with two feet and a serpentine tail

yale: a heraldic beast resembling an antelope with tusks and curved horns, always shown parted

PICTURE ACKNOWLEDGEMENTS

While every attempt has been made by the author and publishers to credit sources correctly, any further information would be welcome.

AKG London: pp36bl, Erich Lessing; 40t; 42b, British Library, from Rothschild Bequest; 50bl, Erich Lessing, Warsaw Museum; 54tr, Erich Lessing; 58br, Domingie Museo Nazionale del Bargello, Florence, Italy; 104tr, British Library; 106b, British Library, Froissart's Chronicle. **Ancient Art & Architecture Collection:** pp11br; 13tl, R. Sheridan; 107br. **Anness Publishing Ltd,** courtesy Daniel de Bruin, photography Jos Janssen: pp38t&bl; 73b; 80tr&bl; 88tl; 111tr. Anness Publishing Ltd/Stephen Slater, photography Mark Wood: pp10b; 21b; 22t; 32t; 32bl, King René's Tourney Book; 38t; 49t; 53t; 58t&bl; 60bl,bm&br; 61bl&tr; 62ml; 64t; 66&85tl; 70tr; 84bl; 86ml; 87tl; 88tr; 98t&bl; 108tr; 109 all; 110bl; 111ml; 116b; 117br. Anness Publishing Ltd/unattributable: pp52tr&br; 53m; 55bl. **Archive of Stato di Massa, Ministero peri Beni le Attivita Culturali,** photograph Progra Immagini, Massa: p87br. **Art Archive:** pp13tr, Manesse Codex, University Library Heidelberg/Dagli Orti; 20t, British Library; 16t, Musée des Arts Décoratifs, Paris/Dagli Orti; 19b, engraving by Hogenberg/Dagli Orti; 20t, British Library, from Roman de Petit Jean de Saintre; 22b, Musée de Versailles/Dagli Orti, copy of anonymous painting at Hampton Court, Friedrich Bouterwick; 24bl, British Library; 39t, Bibliothèque Nationale, Paris; 40br, College of Arms/John Webb, designed by Maximilian Colt, the King's Carver. **Bridgeman Art Library:** pp15t, British Library, Froissart's Chronicle; 18t, British Library; 18b, British Library, Book of Hours; 34br, William Henry Pyne, Herald, from Costume of Great Britain, William Miller, 1805; 39b, Victoria & Albert Museum, T. Rowlandson and A. C. Pugin; 41b, Bibliothèque Nationale, Paris, Chronicle of Charles VII of France. **The College of Arms, London:** p34bl. **Corbis:** p37t. **Edimedia:** pp12t, Chronicle of William of Tyr; 12b, British Library; 14b; 20b; 52tl. **Eglinton County Park/North Ayrshire Council:** p23t&b. **Sonia Halliday Photography:** pp15bl, Church of St Chad, Prees, England, Laura Lushington; 94t, Laura Lushington. **Hulton/Getty:** p59tr. **Willem Jörg:** pp30; 44bm. **A.F. Kersting:** p21, Temple Church, London. **Peter Newark's Pictures:** pp16m; 51tr, Codex Balduineus. **Northern Territories of Australia Government:** p63tr. **Novosti** (London): p36br. **Royal Armouries:** p16bl, IV600. **Salisbury and South Wiltshire Museum:** p24tl. **Scala:** pp13b; 16br; 19t; 28t; 99tl. **Stephen Slater:** pp6; 9b; 10tr; 24br; 25b, Priory Church, Abergavenny, Wales; 26br; 37bl,bm&br; 41tl, Brunswick Cathedral, Germany; 41tr; 42t, Harefield Church, Middx, England; 43t&b, courtesy of the Earl of Rothes and Clan Leslie; 44t, Bruges, Belgium; 44bl, Boyton Church, Wilts,

England; 48 all; 52bl, Salisbury Cathedral, England; 55tl; 60t, Trowbridge Church, Wilts, England; 62tl&br; 64bl; 69bm; 83bl, Salisbury Cathedral, England; 86bl; 87bl, Abbey of St Denis, Paris; 90tm; 95m&bl; 105tl; 108bl; 108br, West Lavington Church; 110tm; 111tl&bl; 112tr; 112bl, Harefield Church, Middx, England; 113ml, Westbury Church, Wilts, England; 113bl; 117bl; 119tl; 120tr; 121tl; 122t; 123tl, tr, ml&bl. **Stockczech:** p83bm, Karla Koruna. **Swiss National Museum,** Zurich: p17tl. **Victoria & Albert Museum:** pp36t, Daniel McGrath; 61br. **Zeiner, Josef:** p82br. **Private Collections:** pp85bl, Marco Foppoli; 62tr, Lord Hanson; 113t, Robert Harrison; 55tr, Jan Van Helmont Publishing Company, Belgium/a European Noble Gentleman; 105bl, Denis E. Ivall;

117bm, Baz Manning; 25tl, Collection of the Duke of Northumberland; 114, private collection; 102br, Carl Stiernspetz; 70bl, Derek Walkden.

Unattributable: pp8tm&rb; 9tl, from John of Worcester's Chronicle; 9r; 11t&rml; 14t&rm; 17b; 25tr; 26t&bl; 27tl; 27b; 28br&bl; 28m, Matthew Paris, Chronicle Majora; 29t, Sir Thomas Wriothesley's Book of Standards; 33 all; 34t, Thomas Jenyns' Ordinary; 36ml; 38br; 40br; 44br; 49b; 50t,bm&br; 54bl; 56t; 56b, Biblioteca Trivulziana; 57bl; 59bl; 63bl; 65bl; 69br; 75bl&br; 82tr, Zurich Roll; 82bl; 84tl, Ripon Cathedral, Yorks, England; 88bl; 99tl&tr; 91br; 92bl; 98bl, Buckland Abbey, Devon, England; 100tr; 102bl; 107tr; 108m; 119tm; 120bl&br; 121tr, ml&bl; 122b; 123br.

Artworks: Marco Foppoli: pp27tr; 29tr; 46 & 65tl; 65tr&br; 75tl; 81 all; 83tl&br; 89br; 96&105tr; 99tr; 101t. Roland Symons: p35 all. Alfred Znamierowski: pp8tr; 15br; 29m; 32br; 45 all; 51tl; 53b & box; 54br; 57m&rt; 59tl; 60ml; 62bl; 63tl&bl; 64bm&br; 68 all; 69t&rm; 71 all; 72 all; 73t; 74; 76 all; 77 all; 78 all; 79 all; 82tl&rm; 84bm&br; 85tr, mr&br; 86tr&br; 87tr; 88mr&br; 90tl, tr, bl, bm &br; 91ml, bl, tr&tm; 92tl, tr&br; 93 all; 94bl, bm&br; 95tl, tm, tr &br; 98mr; 99bl&br; 100br; 101b; 102t; 103 all; 104ml, bl&bm; 107tr&bl; 110tr&bm; 113br; 115; 116t; 117t; 118 all; 119bl, bm, br.

AUTHOR'S ACKNOWLEDGEMENTS

For making this book possible and for the hospitality always shown to me, Steve and Kate Friar. For the inspiration to follow the project through, Arnold Rabbow of Braunschweig. To Arnaud Bunel, Sebastian Nelson and Peter Taylor for help with parts of the text. Thanks to William and Mrs Sybil O'Neill for the kindness in allowing me at all times to make use of Terry's library. Joan Robertson, Karen and John Say, and Margaret Smith for their companionship in the many hours I have bored them silly over escutcheons and hatchments. Baz Manning, without whose help and kindness I would have been unable to complete such a project. Mikhail Medvedev of St. Petersburg for his answering my many questions on Russian heraldry. Alice Hall for her translating letters to foreign locations. Roland Symons for his delightful and unfailing assistance.

Sr Marco and Sra Lia Foppoli for their long and happy friendship. James and Mrs Cathy Constant for the refuge they so often afford me. Robert Harrison for his unstinting encouragement. Sebastian Nelson, a true friend of heraldry from the United States. The Officers of Arms, College of Arms, London for their kindness and expertise in answering many a curious and obscure question. David Hubber with many thanks for his kindness and his artwork. The staff at QinetiQ Larkhill, most especially Andy Pike for his patience and understanding. Joanne Rippin of Anness Publishing, whose patience and tenacity have largely been responsible for making sure this work became a reality and Beverley Jollands for her excellent copy editing. Russ Fletcher for the use of his library. Mrs Manning for her excellent deciphering of my scatty notes. Daniel de Bruin for his

kindness in giving me access to his splendid collection of grants/patents of arms. Veneta Bullen for finding some of the more obscure pictures.

Thanks also to the following people and organizations for help with information or images: Peter Trier of Warpool Court Hotel, St David's; Lt Colonel Herbert A. Lippert (Retd); Mrs Malina Sieczkowska; Michael Messer; Anthony Ryan; the Staff of HM Security Service; The Central Intelligence Agency of the United States, John Uncles; HH the Prince of Oettingen; Herr Willem Jorg; Herr Gunter Mattern; Anthony Jones; Colonel Carnero, Military Attache, Spanish Embassy, London; Risto Pyykko; Keith Lovell; Gordon and Jean Ashton; Bruce Patterson, Saguenay Herald and the Canadian Heraldic Authority; Micheal O'Comain, Consulting Herald, Office of the Chief Herald of Ireland;

Fergus Gillespie, Deputy Chief Herald of Ireland; Elisabeth Roads, Lyon Clerk and the staff of the Court of Lord Lyon, Edinburgh; Andrew Martin Garvey; Jennifer Marin, Curator, The Jewish Museum, London; Dr Adrian Ailes; Mrs Marian Miles OBE, Distributed Technology Ltd, Robin Lumsden; Dame Stephanie Shirley DBE, and the staff of the Prior's Court Foundation; Adjutant Luc Binet and the staff of the Service Historique de l'Armee de Terre, Vincennes; Dr. Jan Erik Schulte, Kultur/Kreismuseum, Buren; Bruce Purvis; Martin Davies; David Phillips; Dr Malcolm Golin; The staff of the Haermuseet, Oslo; Lt. Colonel Nick Bird OBE, RA (Retd) and staff of the Royal School of Artillery; Kevin Fielding; Per Nordenval, Riddarhuset, Stockholm; Anna Lilliehöök, KMO.

And finally, to all bonacons, wherever they may be.

INDEX